The
Shining
Sword

The Shining Sword

Charles G. Coleman

LOIZEAUX BROTHERS
Neptune, New Jersey

THE SHINING SWORD
Charles G. Coleman

First Edition, April 1956
Illustrated Edition, July 1988
Illustrations by Joe VanSeveren

Printed in the United States of America.

A publication of Loizeaux Brothers, Inc., a nonprofit organization devoted to the Lord's work and to the spread of His truth.

Library of Congress Cataloging-in-Publication Data

Coleman, Charles G.
    The shining sword.

    Summary: A young man named Lanus enters the service of the King and must defeat the Enemy in this allegorical portrayal of the Christian's conflict with Satan and the importance of the word of God.
    (1. Allegories. 2. Christian life—Fiction)
I. Title.
PS3553.047384S5   1988   813'.54 (Fic)   88-697
ISBN 0-87213-085-1 Cloth
ISBN 0-87213-086-X Paper

Dedicated to Kit, whose help and inspiration made this book possible.

Contents

The
Shining
Sword

1

The King's Messenger

Below us the land lies bright and warm and peaceful. We are standing, you and I, on a high grassy knoll, with the spring sun warm on our backs and arms, and a pleasant breeze blowing against our cheeks. The knoll rises from about the center of a wide valley. From its foot the patterns of fields and villages and pastureland stretch away eastward and westward to great mountain ridges which rise against the sky.

The valley is called broad valley by its inhabitants and it lies in the land of man. Do not look for it on your map, for you will not find it there. We have come here because this valley and these mountains are the scenes of the story I am about to tell you, a story of some of the people who live in this land. You will find, I am sure, that they are much like people who live in your own country, and perhaps even in your own neighborhood.

Not far from us, in the soft grass on top of the knoll, lies a young man of about eighteen years. He is sprawled at full length on his side, his head pillowed on his arm, looking lazily over the fields below. He is very comfortable. There is work to be done in those fields, but he is not worried about that. He would much rather spend the long afternoon lying in the sun.

I am sorry to say, this young man has few of the admirable qualities we like to find in our friends, but we must get acquainted with him, nevertheless, for interesting things are about to happen to him. His name is Lanus, and he is a principal figure in our story. Come with me to where he lies, for with his first move the story begins.

*   *   *

Lanus yawned, raised himself on one elbow, and cocked an eye at the sun. It was past mid-afternoon, he decided, and nearly time for him to leave the hilltop if he were to reach the village in time for the evening meal. He looked down at the valley, idly watching the movements of tiny black specks in the green fields below. Each of those specks, Lanus knew, was a man. What fools they were, he thought, to slave in the fields when the afternoons were so sunny and warm and the grass on the hilltop so soft!

As you have guessed, Lanus was lazy. He was a tall, strong young fellow, who was always ready for a wrestling bout or a swim, but who found the idea of work very disagreeable. Ever since his parents had died, he had lived a careless, shiftless life, working when he had to, sleeping in barns and haymows, and drifting from farm to farm in the valley. He was not well thought of by the people of broad valley, but they were glad enough to hire him when he chose to work, for no one else would work for such small wages. And many of them were softhearted enough to give him a meal and a place in their barns to sleep when he needed it.

Suddenly Lanus's eye was caught by a new movement below. Someone was coming along the path near the foot of the knoll. Lanus grunted in surprise and sat up. Who beside himself would be coming to such an out-of-the-way place? As the stranger began climbing the slope toward him, Lanus saw that he was fair-haired, and that he wore a long traveling cloak buttoned tightly up the front. There was something about the figure that was familiar. Someone he had known walked in just that way—but who? Then suddenly he remembered. He jumped to his feet and went down the slope with long strides to meet the stranger.

"Robin!" he cried, seizing the other's hand, "where on earth did you come from?"

"Hello, Lanus."

The fair-haired young man smiled and pumped Lanus's hand warmly. He was a stockily built youth, almost but not quite as tall as Lanus, with an open, pleasant face. When the first greetings were over Lanus said, "But Robin, where have you been? You went from the village more than a year ago, just when everyone thought you were on your way to a farm of your own. Folks have been wondering about it ever since."

Robin's face sobered. "I've had a wonderful year, Lanus, a very wonderful year," he said. "I'd like to tell you about it. But there is something more important I must do first." He put his hand on

Lanus's shoulder. "I have a message to deliver."

"What do you mean?"

"I've come looking for you, Lanus. I have an invitation for you!"

"An invitation? From whom?"

"An invitation from the King!"

Bewildered, Lanus stared at his friend. "Are you crazy, Robin? You know we have no king here in the valley. We don't believe in kings. We're independent." He said this last rather proudly, for it was one of the phrases which all of the valley folk were fond of repeating.

Robin smiled sadly and shook his head. "You are wrong, Lanus. There is a King—a great and good and wise King about whom the people of broad valley have forgotten. It is He who watches over and protects the valley, yet He is not acknowledged nor thanked."

Lanus frowned, for what Robin was saying was new to him. "Do you know this King then, Robin?" he asked.

"I know Him," said Robin, and his eyes flashed proudly. "I know Him and I wear His uniform!"

He unbuttoned his long traveling cloak and threw it back from his shoulders. Lanus's eyes opened wide in amazement, for the sunlight glittered on the polished steel surface of a suit of armor. It was wonderfully made. Over Robin's shoulders and chest was a shirt of flexible chain mail in which was set a steel breastplate. Steel plates guarded his hips and thighs. From one side of his belt hung a silver helmet; from the other was suspended a straight, silver-handled sword, while above his shoulder could be seen the top of a shield which was slung on his back.

Lanus whistled softly. "That is quite an outfit,

12

Robin. But say, I've heard about armor like that. I've been told there is a strange sort of tribe in the mountains, the followers of some queer belief, who dress like that. Don't tell me," here a note of scorn crept into his voice, "don't tell me you've joined up with anything like that!"

Robin nodded. "Yes, that's where I've been for the past year. I know some of the folk in the valley make fun of us, but believe me, Lanus, it is the only life worthwhile."

Lanus looked at him doubtfully. "Well, you always have been a levelheaded fellow, Robin, and not one to be carried away with foolish ideas. Perhaps there is something in what you say. I'd like to hear more about it."

"Fine," said Robin, smiling happily. "Sit down and I'll tell you the whole story."

They dropped down on the grass, Robin sitting upright with his arms across his knees, Lanus sprawling characteristically on his back with a piece of grass in his mouth. And Robin told his story. . . .

*   *   *

"A year ago," began Robin, "I worked for Farmer Hanna on the north side of the village. He was a good employer and paid good wages. I liked working in the fresh air and the sunny fields, and hoped someday to save enough to buy a farm of my own.

"But I was not entirely happy. I wondered why, for I could think of nothing I wanted more than to be a successful farmer here in the valley. But it bothered me that all about me were such things as sickness and trouble and discontent. How could anyone be really happy? Even rich and suc-

13

cessful people seemed to have troubles. And always, everywhere in the valley there were quarrels and fights. That was the year, you remember, when war broke out among several of the villages."

"Some of them are still fighting," put in Lanus, chewing his grass stem thoughtfully. Robin nodded, then went on.

"I wondered why it was that we couldn't live peaceably together without selfishness, quarrels, or wars. None of us want such things but they come just the same. So I asked the wise men of my village what were the causes of these evils. Each of them had a different answer. Some said it was just human nature. Others said that mankind hadn't advanced quite far enough yet to solve these problems. Still others said that all we needed was a different sort of government. None of them really knew.

"In the evening when my work was done, I used to walk out under the stars, trying in my mind to find answers to my questions. Where did evil come from? Who began it? And why did evil things happen in our valley? Sometimes as I walked, I would look up at the great mountains towering far above me on either side of the valley. If I were on the mountaintop looking down, I wondered, would I be able to see things more clearly? Perhaps, up there where the air was clear, and the whole valley spread out before me, I could begin to understand the real meaning of life.

"As I thought these things, evening after evening, a great desire grew in me to climb the mountain ridge and look over the valley from the top. I was ashamed to tell my friends of my idea, for I felt they might laugh at me. No one from the valley ever climbed the great mountains.

"I decided to go alone and to tell no one. So when a day came on which I had no important duties, I got up early, asked Mrs. Hanna to pack a lunch for me, and set out for the mountains. I had no idea which part of the great mountains to climb, so I walked generally eastward from the village. But I soon felt my feet turning toward one particular point at the foot of the mountain slope, almost as though someone were leading me by the hand. When I reached the valley's edge, I was surprised to find, directly in front of me, a well-worn path leading up into the mountains. Something within told me that this was the way to go.

"The path drew me along like a magnet, and the pull grew stronger as I climbed. I found myself wondering breathlessly what lay around each new turn of the way. Finally, when I had gone nearly halfway up the mountainside, I saw that the path ahead plunged into a dark wood. As I wondered whether, after all, I should follow this mysterious pull into the dark shadows of the trees, I suddenly saw the figure of a man sitting on a fallen log at the forest's edge. At the same time the man seemed to see me, for he rose to his feet and came forward.

"He was dressed in armor, as I am now, and he smiled at me in a friendly way as he approached. 'Hello, Robin' he said, 'I've been waiting for you.'

"At the look of astonishment on my face, he smiled still more broadly. 'I see you are wondering how I know your name, and how I knew you were coming when you had told no one.' When I nodded, he went on, 'It was not I, Robin, but my Master who knew these things. He sent me here to meet you and bring you to His castle!'

" 'But who is your master, and how can he know me?' I asked.

" 'My Master is King of kings and Lord of lords. His eyes are in every place, beholding the evil and the good. Your ways are not hid from Him, Robin, and He has, for many months, been drawing you to Himself. Come, let us start for the castle, for we have still a long way to go.' "

"As in a dream I followed him into the forest. A long way he led me, up steep slopes and past great rocks, until at last we reached a high stone wall on the mountain ridge. Here a gate was opened and I entered into the King's castle."

"In that castle, Lanus, I had my questions answered for the first time. I learned the real meaning of good and evil. I learned why the valley is torn with wars, and why there is hatred and death. And I found the only life worth living. I stayed in the castle, Lanus, because I had no wish to return to the valley. I stayed and became a soldier of the King!"

*   *   *

Robin fell silent. After a moment, Lanus asked, "And did you see the King, Robin?"

"I have never seen Him, Lanus," replied Robin softly, "for He is not seen with human eyes. But I know Him. I know Him through the book which He has written, and through His sword that I bear. And I know Him because He guides and directs my way. And Lanus, He wants you to know Him, too. He calls you, as He calls everyone in Broad Valley, to come to Him and live.

"He has said, '*I am the resurrection and the life; he that believeth in Me, though he were dead, yet shall he live, and whosoever liveth and believeth in Me shall never die.'* That, Lanus, is your invitation."

*   *   *

For a few moments both lads sat in silence. The sun had just touched the edge of the western mountains, sending the first red streaks of sunset across the sky. Overhead a great hawk swept noiselessly toward his night roost on the mountain slopes. When Lanus finally spoke there was something like awe in his voice.

"Those are strange words, spoken by that King of yours," he said, "yet there is power in them. Do you really believe these things you have told me?"

"With all my heart," answered Robin simply.

"Well," said Lanus thoughtfully, "perhaps I will accept your invitation. I would like to spend a day with you at this castle and see for myself what has changed you."

"Good. Are you ready to start?"

"Now?" Lanus stared at his friend in amazement. Then he laughed. "Robin, you certainly don't waste time. All right, there is nothing to keep me in the village tonight, and certainly no one to miss me if I go. I'm ready if you are!"

2
A Fight on the Path

Robin led the way down from the knoll, and struck off eastward across the valley toward a jutting spur of the great mountains. At first the way led between cultivated fields, but two hours of walking took them away from civilization into rolling grassland. Once they stopped by a small stream long enough to eat some bread and cheese which Robin carried in a package under his cloak, then they went on again. The evening was cool and pleasant, and the two friends found many things to talk about. Lanus told Robin all the news of the valley, and asked many questions about Robin's life as a soldier of the King. And all the time he was watching Robin closely, trying to determine just what change had come over his friend. For Robin had changed. Lanus could see it. He was more mature, more steady, and . . . yes, happier. There was no question about it, this was a new Robin, and the change was for the better.

Shortly after nightfall the moon came up, making the way almost as bright as though it were broad daylight. They were nearing the first hills now, and were drawing close to the towering mountain spur which extended out into the valley. Robin struck upward on a path over the first ridge of foothills, then up the slope of the mountain itself. There was no talking now, for breath was needed for climbing. When they reached the thick woodland, where the moonlight shone through only in patches, Robin stopped, put on his helmet, moved his shield into position, and drew his sword. Then with Lanus close at his heels, he moved ahead through the dark forest.

Once under the trees, Lanus was surprised to find that the path ahead was lit by a strange glow, and it was a few moments before he realized that this light came from the sword which Robin held in front of him like a torch. Although the sword itself did not shine, a soft, steady light illuminated everything around it.

On they went, following the winding path. Sometimes it twisted through areas of heavy undergrowth, or around the trunks of huge trees which towered up into the darkness; at other times it ran past giant boulders. And always the way was upward. Lanus's legs became more and more tired, and his breath came in short gasps, but Robin's pace never slowed. Not wanting to admit his weakness, Lanus gritted his teeth and kept on.

As they were passing a particularly large rock whose face rose sheer from the side of the path, Lanus, looking down into the dark woods on the other side, saw a sight which made him catch his breath in amazement. There, just a few steps away in a small hollow lit by the moonlight, was a beautiful pool of water with smooth grassy banks. To Lanus, tired and thirsty from the climb, that soft grass seemed more inviting than any bed he had ever seen. If only he could rest there just for a minute or two! Certainly there would be no harm in that.

Lanus stopped. "Robin, turn aside just for a moment, will you, and let me get a drink from that pool over to the right?" he called, at the same time starting off the path.

Robin was beside him in a flash. "No!" he cried sharply, "it's a trap! Get back to the path, Lanus, before it is too late!" Lanus stopped, undecided, and at the same instant from the darkness around them came a high-pitched howling noise as of a high wind. Robin threw himself in front, shouting, "Back, Lanus, back!"

Robin raised the sword high and, by its light, Lanus saw something large and shadowy move in the darkness beneath the trees. He tried to scramble up on to the path again, but the bank broke under him. Then he heard Robin give a ringing shout—"For the King!"—and turned to see his friend fighting fiercely against two huge manlike creatures in black armor who slashed at him with swords.

Lanus was no coward. When he saw his friend in trouble, he seized a heavy branch that lay near and rushed forward, aiming a blow at the nearest monster. But to his surprise, the club glanced harmlessly off the creature, who did not even appear to notice it!

"Get back," Robin shouted through clenched teeth. "Nothing can harm them except the sword.

Get back on the path while I hold them off!"

Lanus turned and, with the aid of the branch, scrambled up the bank on to the path. Then Robin, with a mighty effort, drove his assailants backward a few feet and, while they faltered, broke away and dashed for the path. Lanus reached for his hand and pulled him up the bank just before the monsters reached him.

Then, as Lanus stood helplessly against the rock, a desperate battle took place. Robin, standing firmly at the edge of the bank, again and again beat back the rush of his enemies. To Lanus it was like a scene from a nightmare. In his ears rang the howling of winds, though no wind blew. Over Robin's shoulder he could see the snarling faces of the creatures and the heave of their huge shoulders above the black shields as they rushed, time after time, up the slope, only to be met and driven back by Robin's flashing sword. But how long could Robin hold out?

During a lull in the fight, Robin pulled from beneath his cloak a small silver trumpet and hastily blew a high, clear note. At the sight of the trumpet the monsters fell back for a moment, then rushed again with renewed fury. After what seemed hours, Lanus heard a far-off answering note. Then a pale glow shone far up the mountainside, and into view came several men in armor, the light from their swords illuminating the dark wood. As they drew near, Robin's two assailants ceased their attacks and melted back into the shadows of the wood. The weird howling noise died away. To Lanus's surprise, the moonlit clearing and the beautiful pool of water disappeared as well, leaving nothing but darkness. Robin leaned on his sword, panting with exhaustion, as the group of rescuers reached them. The soldier in charge, a tall, powerfully-built man, gave a crisp order, and several of the soldiers climbed down the bank and fanned out, probing the shadows under the trees with their sword-lights.

"It looks as though we got here in time," said the leader, turning to Robin. "Are you two all right?"

Robin straightened up and smiled. "Quite all right, sir." He caught Lanus's arm and drew him forward. "Sir, this is Lanus, my friend from the valley. Lanus, this is Gayne, one of the leaders of our fellowship."

Gayne shook Lanus's hand heartily. "We came down the slope from the watchtower on the ridge above," he explained, "as soon as we knew you were in difficulty. The enemy has been active of late, and we have been expecting some trouble of this sort." He turned back to Robin. "I see you are rested somewhat, Robin. Let us start for the castle. If we wait here, the evil ones may return with reinforcements."

Quickly the little group formed into marching order and, with Lanus and Robin in the center, moved up the path. A short time later they came out of the forest onto the open mountain crest. There along the ridge to the left was a high stone wall, topped by the towers and battlements of a great castle. Lookouts were apparently awaiting their coming, for, as they approached the wall, there were noises from within and a huge, iron-bound gate swung open. As they passed through, the moonlight caught the words of an inscription cut in the stone arch above the gate. Lanus read: *"Knock and it shall be opened unto you."*

While he wondered whether this was another of

the King's sayings, the party moved on across a level grassy yard toward the entrance to the castle itself. There, after following Robin through a long corridor, Lanus found himself in a large, lighted room with a high, vaulted ceiling. In the center of this room a large company of men and women sat around a long, oaken table. Robin led Lanus to the head of the table where a kindly-faced man with white hair rose to meet them.

"Greetings, Latta," said Robin respectfully. "This is my friend Lanus who has come to visit us."

"Well done, Robin," said the old man. "You have not failed in your mission. And to you, young man, a welcome to our home. Here are seats for you both at the table. You are probably hungry after your journey. After you have eaten, Lanus, Robin will show you your room for the night."

The two lads sat down and ate a hearty meal. The food was different in taste from any that Lanus had ever eaten, but it was very good. Afterward Robin took him to a small but comfortable bedroom high in the castle. There, in spite of the excitement of the evening, Lanus fell asleep five minutes after Robin left him.

3
The Castle

When Lanus awoke, the birds were singing cheer-
fully outside his window, the sun was making
bright patterns on the floor, and a short, fat man
was sitting comfortably on the foot of his bed!
While Lanus blinked in surprise, wondering whether this visitor was part of a dream, the man smiled
at him, a broad, happy smile that looked quite at
home on his round face.

"Good morning, Lanus," he said, "you have slept
late. The sun has been up for two hours or more,
and breakfast is waiting for you below."

Lanus grinned in return, stretched, and swung
his legs over the side of the bed. The short man
went on. "My name is Jamin. I am the seneschal
of the castle—the one who takes care of food,
clothing, and other everyday matters for the
King's soldiers. Your friend Robin had to leave early this morning for duty on the eastern ridge, but

I'll look after you while he's gone."

When Lanus had washed and dressed himself, Jamin led him to the great vaulted dining room where he ate a hearty breakfast. After breakfast, Jamin took him to the top of one of the castle towers. From this point the view was breathtaking. Far below was the green grassy area of the castle yard across which moved the tiny figures of men and women. Around the yard rose the outer wall, topped with battlements where lookouts kept their watch. Beyond the wall, on three sides of the castle, wooded ridges of the great mountains stretched away into the distance. On the fourth side, the wooded slopes dropped away to the expanse of broad valley with its checkered pattern of fields and villages.

Lanus saw that the ridge, on which the castle stood, extended westward out into the valley. Along the side of this ridge, he could see, winding downward into the trees, the path up which he had come the night before. In the thickly wooded part of the slope, the path was completely hidden by the foliage, but in other areas he could catch glimpses of it between the treetops.

Jamin pointed downward. "Our lookouts on the wall can keep watch over any of our soldiers who may be traveling the path from the valley. If their journey is at night, we can see the glow from their swords even through the treetops, and tell at once if anything is wrong."

"How?" asked Lanus.

"By the swordlight. When the enemy is near, the light of the sword always flares high, warning the soldier of trouble to come."

"But," asked Lanus, "doesn't the swordlight also tell the enemy where you are? Wouldn't it be better to travel in darkness and slip past him unobserved?"

"You don't know our enemies very well," said Jamin with a smile. "They can see in the darkness far better than we can, for they are creatures of darkness. But they cannot see the light which the sword sends forth. That light is invisible to them. Nor can they hear the notes of the silver trumpet, for the King planned it so."

Lanus looked down again at the sunlit treetops. Even with the memory of last night fresh in his mind, it was hard to believe that deadly enemies lurked in the shadows beneath those trees. He turned back to Jamin. "Were you watching us last night?" he asked.

"Our lookouts saw you. And when the light flared from Robin's sword we knew the enemy was attacking. Soon afterward Robin's trumpet call was heard in the watchtower on the ridge." Jamin pointed once more, and Lanus, looking out along the ridge toward the valley, saw, on a high rocky point overlooking the path, a circular gray stone fortress, around whose walls moved figures in the uniform of soldiers of the King.

"That fortress is our most important post," continued Jamin, "for it keeps the way open to the valley. If the enemy could ever capture and hold it, he could control the path and stop us from carrying out our great mission—that of telling the people of broad valley about the King."

"Does the enemy attack it often?" asked Lanus.

"In the early days of the faith, he laid siege to it many times. In recent years he has not often attacked it in force, preferring to harry us in other ways. As you can see, the approach to the fort from this end of the ridge is well protected by the castle. At the far end of the ridge, where it drops off into the valley, are great cliffs, which form a natural barrier. The sides of the ridge are very steep and difficult to climb. It is not hard for rescue parties from the ridge to make their way down these slopes to the path when travelers are in trouble there, but it would be difficult for war parties of the enemy to climb them in enough force to capture the tower."

Lanus looked thoughtfully out over the valley. "Tell me, Jamin," he asked, "why don't you tell the valley folk about these evil ones? They might help you to fight them."

Jamin shook his head. "The evil ones can't even be seen without the sword, Lanus. The people of broad valley have been told about the evil ones—they have the work of the evil ones all about them—but because they can't see they won't believe. Why, Lanus, the evil ones have ruled over the whole valley for years without being found out!"

"They don't rule over the village where I live," said Lanus stoutly. "We are independent and rule ourselves."

Jamin smiled but his eyes were kind. "The influence of the evil ones is there. Tell me, lad, are there discontented people in your village?"

"Well . . . yes, there are. Some are discontented because they want more money, and some because they want a different village government, and some for other reasons, but that you find in any village."

"And have you wars in your village?" pursued Jamin.

"We have had many wars with other villages. Now we are at peace, but we fear we may be

30

attacked soon and are preparing for it, though we are a peaceful people," replied Lanus.

"And is there thievery and selfishness and hatred in your village?"

"Yes—but there are many good people too."

"And can you—think carefully, Lanus—can you think of one person, just one, in your village who is completely, one-hundred-percent happy and satisfied and contented?"

"Well . . . no."

"Ah, Lanus, the conditions in your village are the work of these same evil ones. They move among you, spreading discontent and keeping your good villagers so busy with wars and troubles that they do not realize that they are under the power of evil. That is why we go to the valley with the message of salvation; for it is only when men and women turn to the King that they find real peace and happiness, and break the hold of evil forever."

Then Jamin turned to the other side of the castle, which overlooked the heavily forested slopes of the great mountains. He began pointing out, on the mountain ridges below, the positions of the outposts which guarded the approaches to the castle from all directions.

"Each of these posts," he said, "has its own area to guard and control. Each has its part to play in keeping the enemy from breaking through in force. While small numbers of the enemy still slip through to attack the King's soldiers on the path to the valley, these outposts prevent large war parties from closing the path completely."

For several moments they stood there while Jamin's pointing finger traced out, on the mountaintops below, the carefully-planned pattern of defenses for the castle. Finally Lanus said, "This is wonderful, Jamin, all of it. And the castle is the most wonderful of all. Did your King build it?"

"It was He who planned it and who laid the foundation of the building. The ground had already been cleared and prepared by such ancient warriors as Moses and David and Isaiah, whom the King had sent before to prepare for His coming. But these men did not know the King's design for the castle itself.

"Then the King came to the valley and with His own hands laid the foundations of the castle. And before He went away again, He entrusted the rest of the building to a little group of His followers. These men—Peter, James, John, Paul, and the rest—became the first of the present-day soldiers of the King. They laid courses of stone upon the King's foundation, and fought off the evil ones who tried to hinder the work. Those who followed them built more and more until now the castle is nearly finished."

"Do you mean," asked Lanus, "that all of the King's soldiers are stonemasons as well?"

Jamin laughed. "Yes, stonemasons and many other things beside. We are a busy company."

Lanus was silent for a moment. "Tell me, Jamin," he said at last, "how does one become a soldier of the King? For example, if I wanted to join your fellowship, how would I do it?"

Jamin looked at him seriously. "You could be a soldier of the King only if you believe in Him and are willing to give your life to His service. For He has said: *'If any man will come after Me, let him deny himself and take up his cross daily and follow Me.'* "

Jamin paused while his sharp eyes seemed to

bore through Lanus. Then he said gently, "You really know very little about us, Lanus. This life is a hard one, and there is much work to do. We have no time to loaf or to lie in the sun of a summer afternoon."

Lanus blushed. How much had this shrewd man guessed about his weaknesses, anyway?

Again Jamin flashed his kindly smile. "Let me show you more of how we live," he said, as he led the way down the winding tower stairs. Through several corridors they went to the castle kitchen, where several men and women were busily preparing food for meals to be served later in the day.

"We have no servants," Jamin said, "for the King said when He was here: *'He that is greatest among you, shall be your servant.'* These people are soldiers of the King like the rest of us."

"That is a strange rule," thought Lanus to himself, "and what is even more strange is the way these people quote the King's sayings as though they were their only guides."

Out through a door into the open air they went, to the rear yard of the castle. Here, in large gardens, other men and women were hard at work between the rows of growing things. "This too," said Jamin, "is work which must be done each day. Preparing food for the soldiers of the King is a most important duty."

Then Jamin led the way back into the castle and through more passages to the unfinished section of the building, where several soldiers were at work trimming, smoothing, and laying the stonework on a partly-erected castle tower. Stripped to the waist and wet with perspiration, they tugged and lifted the huge stones into position, spread and smoothed the mortar, and finished the joints.

"This work," said Jamin, "is shared by every soldier. It is not as exciting as fighting with the enemy, but it is very necessary. For when the castle is finally finished, the King will return to the valley again. Every stone that we lay is bringing that time nearer."

As they left the stonemasons, Lanus asked, "Why is it, Jamin, that these soldiers wear their swords even when laying stone? Doesn't the extra weight make their work harder?"

And Jamin answered, "We must be ready at all times for the enemy, who often attacks when we least expect him. When the alarm sounds, every soldier must be ready to fight. So, whether we work in the gardens, clean the castle halls, or build the towers higher, we wear our swords, and have our shields and helmets at hand."

By this time they had passed through the castle and reached the grassy yard in front of the main entrance, where two young soldiers were practicing swordsmanship under the direction of an older man.

"One of our most important duties," said Jamin, "is studying the use of our weapons. It takes long hours of practice to become a real swordsman."

They crossed the yard to the gate in the castle wall. "Next I want to show you one of our outposts," Jamin said, as he led the way through the gate. Outside, he skirted the castle wall to the side farthest from broad valley, then struck out along the mountainside, following a well-worn path. A short walk brought them to a clearing where a group of soldiers were busily building higher some earth and timber barricades. As they approached this company, Lanus said suddenly, "Look, there's Robin!"

And sure enough, there he was. His muscles straining and his blond hair shining in the sun, Robin was helping to carry a heavy log from the edge of the wood to a position on one of the barricades. After the log was laid in place, Jamin called to him, and Robin came, brushing the perspiration from his face with the back of his hand. He grinned at Lanus as he came up.

"I'm sorry I haven't been able to be with you, Lanus," he said, "but you see, I'm a woodchopper today."

"Is there this much work to do here every day?" asked Lanus, wondering at the flurry of activity.

"No," replied Robin, "this is rather an emergency. You see, shortly after you and I were attacked on the path last night, the enemy staged a full-scale raid on this outpost and nearly captured it. The detachment on duty beat them off after a stiff fight, but not before the barricades were pretty well destroyed. We must repair and strengthen them today so that, if the enemy attacks again tonight, the post can be defended."

"Is there any connection," asked Lanus, "between the fight you had on the path last night and the attack here?"

This time it was Jamin who answered. "Indeed there is, lad. The enemy dislikes everything we do, but what makes him angriest is when we persuade folk from the valley to visit us. You see, he knows that the people of the valley belong to him, and he fears that if they visit the castle, they may become followers of the King. Now this outpost doesn't protect the path directly, but if the

enemy can damage our defensive line any-
where, he can keep us so busy rebuilding it that
we have no time to visit the valley with invitations
from the King."

"I see," said Lanus. "When the enemy learned
that Robin had brought me from the valley, he
decided it was time to stir up trouble for you."

"That's right," said Robin, "and, as you see, he's
kept ten of us busy all day repairing the damage."

Just then a whistle shrilled from across the clearing. "Sounds as though they are ready for another
log," said Robin. "I must get back to my job. Jamin
will take care of you, Lanus, and I'll see you at the
end of the day." And, with a wave of his hand, he
ran off to join a group at the forest's edge.

Jamin and Lanus stood watching the work for a
few more moments, then turned back toward the
castle. On the way they passed two soldiers carrying large kettles of steaming food toward the
hill they had just left. Jamin turned with a smile.
"You see, Lanus, it is lunch time already. Robin and
his friends will be served at their posts, but there
will be food waiting for us at the castle."

And lunch was indeed waiting for them in the
castle hall. The food was delicious, and Lanus,
who found that the mountain air had made him
hungry, ate heartily. Afterward, with Jamin, he
took a walk through the castle grounds to see the
beautiful flowers and fruits which grew there.
When they returned, Jamin led the way to the
castle library. Here were shelves and shelves of
books filled with writings about the King and the
castle.

"I must go for a while and tend to my duties,"
said Jamin, taking a large book from the shelf. "I

will leave here with you the King's book which will answer many of your questions. This wonderful book was prepared by men under the direction of the King, and is filled with His wisdom. Read it carefully, for its words are words of life!"

When Jamin had left, Lanus found a comfortable chair and began to leaf idly through the book. But soon his attention was caught by the meaning of the words before him. Here in this book was the whole story of the broad valley, of the King, and of the evil ones! Here was just what he wanted to know! Lanus settled down deeper into his chair and began to read in earnest.

4
The Book

Long ago (Lanus read), the valley had all be-
longed to the King. It was a part of His kingdom,
and had been from the beginning of time. But the
Evil One and his followers, who were sworn enemies of the King, wanted the valley for themselves. They came to the valley, deadly and invisible, and, because they were invisible, they were
able to whisper their evil thoughts into the ears of
the first of the valley people.

"Don't serve the King," they whispered, "throw
off His yoke and be independent. Then the valley
will belong to you!" For they knew that if they
could persuade the people to leave the King's
protection, they themselves could become the
rulers of broad valley.

The first of the valley people, not realizing that
they were exchanging their freedom for a terrible
captivity, listened to the whispers of the evil ones,

and rebelled against the King!

Now the King had sworn to destroy all of the evil ones and their works. But still He loved the people of the valley. Because of this love, and because He was merciful, as well as great, He did not punish them for their rebellion. But He sent many messengers to the valley, who called upon men and women in the King's name to turn from their evil ways.

Some of the King's messengers were writers, who wrote of the King's power and glory in stories and prophecies and beautiful verse. Some were speakers, who stood in the village squares and cried to all who would hear, warning of the judgment which would someday fall on the evildoers. And some of the messengers were quiet folk, who went through the villages telling of the King's love and goodness, and pleading with men and women to leave the evil ones and turn again to the King.

The people of the valley, with the whispers of the evil ones in their ears, laughed at the King's messengers. Some of them they killed, and some they put in prison, and some they drove away into the mountains. But always the King sent more. Again and again the messengers came, and again and again they were scorned and persecuted. Some men and women believed the King's message, but these folk too were laughed at by the rest.

Meanwhile the evil ones had built their castles around the valley, and settled down to enjoy the results of their capture. They stole the ripened grain for themselves, and the fruits of the trees in the valley. And all the time they kept the valley farmers so busy hating and fighting and quarreling with one another that they never realized what was happening. The broad valley, which had been a place of peace and contentment, became a valley of unhappiness and ruin.

Finally the King Himself came to the valley. He did not come in power and with armies to destroy the evil ones, for then He would also have had to destroy those who had followed after evil. He came alone, to meet evil face to face, and to vanquish it. For the King understood evil as did no one else. He knew its cruelty, its cunning, its terrible results.

So it was that He came to the valley as a poor carpenter, who went about among the villages doing good. He healed the blind, the lame, and the sick; always He spoke to the people, telling them of His love for them, and asking them to turn from evil and to follow Him. And His goodness, His perfect goodness, shone out through His words and deeds, so that by His life the people of the valley could see how sinful they themselves had become. Almost they repented! Almost they turned again to the King! But the evil ones stirred up the people to anger. "Get rid of this preacher, this good one," they whispered. And once again men listened to the whisperers. Instead of receiving the carpenter as their King, the people of the valley seized Him as a criminal, while His followers ran away in terror. And they put Him to death!

The evil ones had won, it seemed, and the valley would be theirs forever. Sorrowfully a few of the King's friends laid His body to rest in a cave and closed the entrance with a large stone. But the King's power was stronger even than death.

On the third day, the stone was found rolled away, and the grave empty. The King had risen from the dead!

Quickly the news spread, despite the efforts of the evil ones to stop it. The King had risen!

But no longer was He to travel through the valley in humble guise. His work there was finished. Calling His scattered followers together, He told them of the future. And as they listened, they began to understand that the King's death had been part of a great plan—the King's plan—to defeat evil, and to bring to an end the terrible power of the evil ones!

Yes, the King had chosen to die. Long before He came to the valley, He had determined that He must give Himself for the people He loved so well. All of the efforts of the evil ones had only served to bring about the King's own purpose—to die for His subjects. And in a way that man can only partly understand, the King had, by dying, entered into deadly battle with the heart and root of evil to destroy it. His resurrection was proof that He had won that battle. Henceforth those who believed in Him would be made free forever from the power of evil—free to serve the King and to wait for His everlasting kingdom.

When the King's followers understood this, they were filled with joy. Gladly they followed Him to the mountaintop. There on the ridge He showed them a great stone foundation, and told them of the design of the castle which was to be built upon it. Then He gave them His parting gifts. He gave them armor so that they might stand against the attacks of the evil ones. He gave them the sword, sharper than any used by the King's followers in the past, for the power of His resurrection lay within it. And He gave them the silver trumpet, with which they could call upon Him in time of need. And with these gifts He gave them the promise of His own spirit, to be with them, to guide them, and to strengthen them as they fought against the enemy.

And so the King went away. But those He left behind built up, on His foundation and with His guidance, a great strong castle. Boldly they went into the valley, telling people of Him. And many of the valley folk, whose hearts were touched, left all and joined the ranks of His army. And the evil ones found that, against the swords of the King's soldiers, they could do nothing.

So the soldiers of the King worked and fought and waited. For they knew that some day, as He had promised, their Lord would come again to banish evil, to bring joy and peace again to the valley, and to be with His people forever.

*   *   *

The door to the library opened softly. Lanus looked up with a start to see Robin's smiling face framed in the doorway.

"I was afraid I'd find you asleep," said Robin, "Jamin told me he had left you here nearly three hours ago."

Lanus closed the book gently and put it down. His eyes were thoughtful. "No, I haven't been sleeping, Robin. Jamin gave me the King's book to read, and I became so interested that I lost track of the time." He stood up. "It is a wonderful book, Robin; and your King is a wonderful person. I will have much to think about when I get back to the valley."

"There is no need for you to leave soon," said

Robin. "You are welcome to stay here at the castle as long as you like."

Lanus shook his head. "I came for a day's visit," said he, "and to tell you the truth, Robin, if I stay longer, I will find myself wanting to be a soldier too."

"But Lanus, that is just what the King wants you to do—to turn from the valley and its ways and become one of His followers."

Lanus hesitated for a long moment. Then again he shook his head. "This life is not for me, Robin," he said with a shade of regret in his voice. "I am a man of the valley and there I must stay. I like to sleep and play, and work only once in a while. I'm just not cut out to be a soldier of the King." He put his hand on Robin's shoulder. "I've enjoyed this visit more than I can tell you, Robin, and I'm very glad I came. But I must go back to where I belong."

Robin's face showed his disappointment, but he only said, "That is for you to decide, Lanus. But stay with us tonight at least, then I'll see you safely down the path in the morning."

To this Lanus agreed, for he had no wish to travel the path at night. A moment later the dinner bell rang and, arm in arm, the two friends left the library.

5

Storm and Darkness

Early the next morning, Robin and Lanus left the castle and started down the path toward the valley. Even in daylight, the gloom under the trees was so intense that Robin had to use his sword to light the way. However, the path seemed much less terrifying than it had been on the night Lanus had come to the castle.

"Going down the path is seldom dangerous," said Robin when Lanus asked him about this. "You see, the evil ones are only interested in keeping people from coming to the castle."

When they reached the lower edge of the wood, Robin stopped. "You will have no trouble finding your way home from here," he said, "and here I must turn back. But remember, Lanus, the castle gate is always open to you. For the King's word to all is: *'Ask, and it shall be given you; seek, and ye shall find; knock, and it shall be opened unto you.'* Remember that saying, and think well of all you have seen and heard. It may be you will yet turn to the King."

The two friends shook hands warmly. "If the King wills, I will stop to see you on my next trip to the valley," said Robin.

Lanus nodded. Then he turned and went down the path toward the valley. Robin stood for a few moments looking after him, then turned, drew his sword, and disappeared into the shadows of the wood.

*   *   *

Back in the valley again, Lanus dropped easily into his old way of life. None of his friends asked him where he had been, for it was quite usual for Lanus to go off somewhere for several days without telling anyone. Even had they known of his visit to the castle, it is doubtful that they would have seen any change in him. Outwardly he was the same pleasant, indolent young fellow they had known before. He sang and danced and played as he had always done, and he still spent his afternoons on his back on some comfortable, grassy hilltop.

But Lanus did not forget. Often, as the days passed, he thought of the castle and of the men and women who lived there. And, in the evenings, when dusk spread itself across the valley floor and dark shadows fell across his path, he thought of the evil ones.

The evil ones—had he really seen them or only imagined them? Did they, as the King's book said, rule the valley? Were they, even now, near him as he walked the dark path to the village?

He tried to forget these thoughts. None of his acquaintances seemed to worry about such things; why should he? But the harder he tried, the more these questions troubled him. Lanus busied his mind with other things. He laughed louder, played harder. He even worked harder, much to the surprise of his friends. But still the questions came. They filled his daylight hours, and sometimes they kept him awake at night.

One afternoon, tired and troubled, he climbed slowly to the top of the grassy hill where Robin had found him weeks before. There he threw himself down on the grass. If only he could find answers to his questions! Who was right—Robin and Jamin in their mountain castle, or the valley folk in their comfortable farmhouses? If the people of the valley were right, the King's soldiers were fools, throwing their lives away on fables and folklore. If the King's book were true, the valley folk—and Lanus with them—were slaves of an evil power which ruled the valley.

Who was right . . . who? It was an important question, Lanus knew, for his whole life hinged on the answer. His mind went over and over the problem until, tired and discouraged, he began to doze. Then, as he hovered halfway between waking and sleeping, he seemed to see again the gate of the King's castle rising before him. And Robin's words rang in his ears: *"Ask, and it shall be given you; seek, and ye shall find; knock, and it shall be opened unto you."*

Lanus awoke with a start. Had someone just said those words or had he dreamed them? He looked around him, but the hilltop was empty. He said the words over to himself. Perhaps here was his answer. Had not Robin told him that the real meaning of good and evil was only to be learned in the castle?

Suddenly Lanus wanted very much to be again inside the castle. He would go back—to ask his questions, to have his doubts settled one way or another. He looked at the sun. The afternoon was only half gone. If he hurried, he might reach the castle before nightfall.

As Lanus walked rapidly along the road toward the foot of the great mountains, he saw that storm clouds were blowing along the mountain crest. It began to rain as he crossed the foothills, a cold, unpleasant drizzle that soaked his clothes. The sky became more and more overcast as he climbed, until it was nearly as dark as night. Then, just as he reached the lower edge of the forest, there was a flash of lightning, a loud roll of thunder, and the storm broke.

On and upward under the trees plunged Lanus, while the wind blew branches down around him, and torrents of rain pelted the treetops. Water poured down the mountainside too, turning the path into a small stream and swirling around his feet. It was dark in the forest, and the swaying tree trunks were black moving shadows in the gloom. How Lanus wished for Robin's presence by his side, and his sword to light the way!

There was a crash ahead as a great tree went down. It fell across the path, and Lanus had to climb over it, feeling his way through a mass of branches. On the upper side he dropped to the ground and began fighting his way clear of the tangled limbs. Branch after branch he pushed aside, only to find still another against his face. It was not until several minutes later that the truth came to him. it was not tree branches he was fighting, but underbrush. He had lost the path!

He hunted to the left, then to the right, but found only more thickets. Then he turned downhill and tried to find the fallen tree again, but his sense of direction was gone, and he passed it in the darkness. A few more minutes of wandering convinced him—he was lost on the mountainside!

Lanus stopped to think. There were only two directions of which he was sure. If he went up, fighting his way into the storm, he would eventually reach the mountain ridge. Perhaps he would find the castle; perhaps he would miss it in the darkness, and have to spend the night on the open mountainside. Perhaps (and the thought gave him a sinking feeling in the pit of his stomach) if he went on wandering in the mountain, the evil ones which he had seen in this same forest would find him!

He looked down through the darkness. Somewhere below lay the valley, but he had found no answers there. If he turned back now he might never find them. For only a moment more Lanus hesitated. Then, grimly, he turned and faced the slope. It *was* a chance, but maybe one worth taking. With jaw set and shoulders squared, he began again to climb.

Upward he struggled through the night. Sometimes he stood upright, forcing his way step after painful step through the underbrush, while the wild wind whipped branches against his face. Sometimes he crawled on hands and knees, pulling himself up steeper slopes by handholds on trees and bushes. Often vines and roots caught his feet, throwing him down on the muddy ground.

Still he went on, though his breath came in deep sobs, and his arms and legs grew so tired he could hardly lift them. And as Lanus's body struggled through the wet mountain thickets, his mind once more grappled with his great problem.

He thought again of the valley he had left. Like the slowly-turning pages of a picture album, scenes of the past came into his mind. He remembered cool mornings in the fields and the cheerful voices of the farmers as they joked together on their way to harvest the ripened grain. He heard again the evening music of violins on the village green. He saw sunlit streams where he had fished, and shady trees under which he had slept. And, for a moment, he felt again like turning back.

Then he thought of other things he had seen in the valley—of how men loved their lands and gold more than they did their fellowmen, of how they acknowledged no king but their own desires. He saw again the flashing of fists in angry fights, the frowning faces of the discontented, and the thin, wasted forms of the hungry.

In spite of its beauty, there was evil in the valley. Lanus no longer doubted it. And that evil was in the hearts of the people themselves. It was man who was selfish, man who lied and quarreled. And, if the King's book were true, it was man who, when the King came to the valley, had rejected and killed Him!

Of all this Lanus thought, panting upward on the mountainside, with sharp branches tearing at his face and arms, and the soft earth slipping beneath his feet. Then he thought of himself. Was this evil within him as well? After all, he had never done anything really wicked. Deep into his own heart looked Lanus. Laziness was there, and vanity. Selfishness was there, dark as the night around him. He hunted carefully through the past for some sign of goodness within himself—something that would make him worthy of the King's help—but found none. Lanus had lived for his own selfish ends. He had twisted truth to suit his own purposes. He had loved evil.

The howl of the wind grew louder and, in its wailing, Lanus heard the sorrow of the world given voice. And the voice was calling him back from the mountaintop. "The evil is in you!" it seemed to say. "You are ours and you must return!"

The branches became fingers then, pulling at his clothing, dragging him back from the castle to the slavery of the valley. He fought savagely. But the body of Lanus was very tired, and his soul was sick with the understanding of his own sinfulness. And the sharp thorns of the forest seized him and held him fast.

He could climb no farther. He crouched exhausted in the darkness, with the cold rain washing over him and despair in his heart. He would have to turn back. The castle was not for him. With what strength he had left, he would blunder his way back down the mountainside, hoping to reach the valley. There he would live out his life, never again raising his eyes to the mountain.

Words began saying themselves within Lanus's weary mind, words he had heard before: *"Ask, and it shall be given you; seek, and ye shall find; knock, and it shall be opened unto you."*

He shook his head. He had tried and failed. He was beaten. But still the words came: *"Ask, and it shall be given you. . . ."* Wait! That was something he had not done. The thought came slowly. He had been seeking for truth in his own way. He had never asked the King for help! For only a moment his hopes flared high, then the feeling of despair returned. Surely the King would not listen to the prayer of one so undeserving. Still, nothing would be lost by trying. Lanus bowed his head. His mind sought through the empty reaches of space for One to help. And his heart cried out: "Save me! Save me! Lord, Save me!"

He waited hopelessly, seeing nothing, hearing only the howling storm. Then suddenly Lanus began remembering things. No memories of the valley were these thoughts that trooped into his head, but things he had seen and heard at the King's castle. Fragments from the King's great book, phrases from the lips of Jamin and Robin— all came crowding his thoughts. And, as he waited, they fell into place like pieces of a giant jigsaw puzzle, revealing a great and glowing truth that Lanus had somehow, in his struggles, failed to see.

The King loved all the people of the valley. His book said so. And this included Lanus! Though he was unworthy, though he was sinful, the King loved him!

It was the first time Lanus had applied the King's words to himself personally. And the thought was almost too dazzling to grasp. For if he was included in the King's great love, he was also included in the King's salvation. It was as though everyone else had faded away, leaving only Lanus and his King. The King had come to the valley long ago— for Lanus. He had died and risen again—for Lanus. Lanus, the rebel, deserved only death, but the King in wonderful love had died in his place.

How blind he had been! While he had struggled to free himself from the valley by his own efforts, the way, prepared by Another, had been open all the time! He had only to accept the deliverance that the King had provided for him.

Lanus fell on his knees in the thicket. Into his mind came a sentence which Robin had once repeated, a sentence spoken long ago by the King to one who doubted Him: *"I am the resurrection and the life, he that believeth in Me, though he were dead, yet shall he live, and whosoever liveth and believeth in Me shall never die. Believest thou this?"*

And the heart of Lanus, from out of the thorn bush and the storm, breathed out the simple, age-old answer, "Lord, I believe!"

Lanus opened his eyes. Nothing had changed. Nothing. And yet he had been heard; he was sure of it. Then suddenly, while he still knelt, there came a blinding flash of lightning, followed by a terrible thunderclap. Lanus caught his breath. For in the brief flare of light he had seen, only a few steps away, a path and, on ahead, silhouetted against the sky, the friendly turreted outline of the castle wall!

He struggled to his feet. With new strength he tore at the branches which separated him from the path. Then slowly but confidently he felt his way up the path toward the castle. Nothing had changed. The rain still fell and the wind still buffeted him at every step. But the night was somehow warm and friendly. Someone was with him, beside him—Someone strong and holy and infinitely good, Someone to trust, now and forever.

His choice was made. Lanus had taken a stand in the great battle of good and evil—a battle of which he as yet understood little.

Lanus's outstretched fingers touched something

solid. He ran his hands over the rough surface, and traced out the hinge of a great door. *"Ask, and it shall be given you; seek, and ye shall find; knock, and it shall be opened unto you."*

Lanus smiled in the darkness. He had asked and received a new life to be spent in the King's service; he had sought and found a new home of the King's providing. Now he had only to finish the verse.

Still smiling, and with a new peace in his heart, Lanus, servant of the King, knocked boldly at the gate of the King's castle!

6

The King's Armor

Two young soldiers, their shields held high, their swords flashing in the sun, circled each other warily. A little to one side stood Gayne, the swordmaster, watching their movements closely, and calling out instructions now to one, now to the other. It was sword-drill time in the castle yard.

Lanus sat with a group of soldiers on the grass against the castle wall, watching the swordplay. More than any other part of castle life, Lanus enjoyed the long hours of practice with the King's weapons. Even though a number of weeks had passed since the night he became a soldier of the King, he felt that he was only beginning to learn how to use the shield and sword properly. Some soldiers of Lanus's age, like Robin, were already accomplished swordsmen, and Lanus was determined to erase the difference as soon as he could.

His weapons had been given him on the morning after his arrival when Gayne had taken him to the King's armory, deep in the rock beneath the castle. Here he was given new clothing of fine-textured material to replace his own well-worn clothes.

"Those who serve the King," said Gayne, "wear only the clothes that He provides. Nothing that we can bring is suitable to be worn with the King's armor."

Then Gayne brought him a belt, beautifully woven of silver links. From this belt hung a short skirt formed of narrow leaves of steel to protect his hips and thighs. Lanus took the belt in his hands and saw, engraved on the silver buckle, the word *truth.*

"This is the belt of truth," said Gayne. "Care for it well and wear it always. Many times in battle has the belt of truth protected me against the enemy's blows. You see, one good blow at the thighs will so disable a man's legs that he cannot stand, and the best sword arm is of no use without a pair of legs under it. So truth will help you to stand firm, no matter what the attack may be. Without it, the rest of your armor is of little use."

Lanus buckled the belt around him. It fitted perfectly, and seemed to weigh nothing at all. Gayne, noticing his amazement, smiled.

"The belt of truth will bear you up, Lanus, as long as you walk in right paths. If you stray, you will soon have to put it off, for it will be as heavy as lead."

Then Gayne brought a fine coat of mail, in which were set steel plates to protect the chest and shoulders. On the breast, over the heart, was written the word *righteousness.*

"This is the breastplate of righteousness. It protects your heart. The darts of the evil ones are often aimed at the heart, and only the righteousness that the King provides will turn the blows."

Next came a pair of shoes, protected across the instep with steel plates. Everything thus far had had a name, so Lanus looked at the shoes carefully, expecting to see something written on them. And he was not disappointed. Across the top of one was written PREPARE THE WAY and on the other was OF THE LORD, so that when the shoes were set side by side, the complete sentence, PREPARE THE WAY OF THE LORD, could be read.

"These shoes," said Gayne, tapping them with his finger, "were called by the great soldier Paul, 'The preparation of the gospel of peace.' You see, even though we are soldiers, our main job is peace. We fight the evil ones because we must, but we also carry to men the word of truth, telling them of the peace which the King came to the valley to bring, and how they can, by following Him now, come at last to His eternally-peaceful kingdom. The soldier's shoes carry him on these errands. We don't need to travel far to find our enemies, for they are all around us, but we need the King's shoes to carry His message to every corner of the valley."

Like everything else that Gayne had given him, the shoes fit Lanus exactly. While he was fastening them, Gayne went to the back of the armory, and brought out a shield. In the center of the shield was a cross, and on the cross was inscribed in letters of gold the single word, *faith*.

"This is your most important single piece of armor, Lanus, because it is the only one you can shift from place to place. Each of the other pieces will protect the part it covers, but if you had no shield of faith the enemy would quickly find a joint in your armor through which he could send a dart. The shield will turn his blow before it ever reaches your body."

Lanus held the shield so that the light shone on it, then, with a puzzled expression, he rubbed at the surface with his hand.

"Why is it that this shield doesn't shine like Robin's and yours?" he asked. "It looks like the same kind of shield."

"Mine was dull like yours when I first got it," said Gayne, "and so was Robin's. They grew bright as we used them. These are strange and wonderful shields, Lanus. The shields made by men get scratched and battered with use, but not so with these. The more they are used, the brighter they shine! And if I, or any of the King's soldiers, were to fail to use our shields in His service as we should, they would lose their luster and become dull again."

"Well then," said Lanus, "I will hope for an early chance to use my shield, for I want it to shine like yours."

Next Gayne gave him a helmet which protected his head and the sides of his face, and which buckled snugly under his chin. Across the forehead was written the word *salvation*.

"This helmet," said Gayne, "is made of the strongest of materials in the King's domain and will turn the fiercest blow. The enemy knows the helmet well. When he sees it, sparkling above the soldier's shield in battle, it fills him with dismay, for he knows that the great, overhand, crushing blows which he loves are useless to him. The helmet of salvation protects those vital parts which make a soldier what he is—his eyes, to see the way ahead; his ears, to hear the King's commands; and his brain, which directs the movements of his body as he fights the King's battles."

When Lanus had put on the helmet, he stood in complete defensive armor—belt, breastplate, shoes, shield, and helmet. Gayne looked at him approvingly. "Now you look like a true soldier," he said, "but there is something else you need." Once more he disappeared into the shadows in the rear of the room. When he came forward again, he was carrying in his hands the one thing that Lanus had been waiting for above all others. Reverently, Gayne hung it in its place on the belt of truth.

"The sword!" said Lanus, his eyes shining.

"Yes," said Gayne, "the sword. It is known by many names. Soldier Paul called it the 'sword of the spirit, which is the word of God.' And in the King's book we read that it 'pierces even to the dividing asunder of soul and spirit, and of the joints and marrow.' The great warrior David called it 'a lamp unto my feet and a light unto my path.' "

As he spoke, Gayne adjusted the position of the sword so that it hung naturally at Lanus's side. "This sword is your guide and sure defense, your true friend and counselor, and the key to all of the soldier's problems," he said. "Bear it faithfully."

Last of all Gayne brought out a small silver trumpet, like the one Robin had used on the path, and hung it from Lanus's neck by a silver cord. On the trumpet was engraved the word *prayer.* "This is the soldier's help," he said. "Its call will sound for miles across the mountain slopes, bringing you aid when you are alone and outnumbered by your

63

enemies. Best of all the notes of this trumpet are heard by the listening ear of the King Himself, who is quick to help those in need.

"These are your weapons, Lanus. With them you are fully armed and ready for service. May our Lord and King make you ever worthy to bear them."

And Lanus, resting his hand on the silver pommel of the sword, said earnestly, "I hope He will."

But in the weeks that followed, Lanus found that there was a great deal more than hope needed to become a good soldier. There were hours to be spent with Jamin, the seneschal, learning the code of the soldier—how he should conduct himself in the castle and in the field. There were days spent in doing the work of a soldier—helping in the garden, mixing mortar for the stonemasons, or scrubbing and cleaning the rooms and halls of the huge building. There were long afternoons in the library with Wendel, the keeper of the books, studying the wonderful writings of the King. And, of course, there was sword drill.

Sword drill was usually conducted by Gayne in the grassy castle yard. He would line up the young soldiers and make them practice each stroke and parry until they knew them by heart. Then he would let them try these strokes in mock battles between themselves.

Lanus was surprised at first to find that real swords were used in these training battles. But Gayne told him, "The sword is only deadly to the enemies of the King," and Lanus found that it was true. Many times in those early days a well-directed stroke from the sword of one of Gayne's eager young students would find a weak spot in Lanus's defense. Their blows would sting but, sharp though the sword was, it would not cut him. And as time went on, and he studied his faults and corrected them, the blows he received became fewer and fewer.

On this particular afternoon, as he sat against the castle wall, Lanus was feeling pleased with himself. He had already had an hour's practice in the art of catching darts on his shield, and had done well enough to draw a nod of approval from Gayne. Now he was awaiting his turn at sword practice. Finally the bout he was watching was halted by Gayne, who called the whole group around him.

"I hope you all were paying close attention," he said. "That was a fine passage at arms. Robin, your swordplay was excellent, but try for a little more variation in your strokes. Del, your handling of the shield of faith would have done credit to Latta himself.

"Now you two rest and clean your weapons. The rest of you pair off and practice strokes and parries. I," he adjusted his helmet and picked up his shield, "will trade blows with Lanus, here!"

Lanus was surprised and excited. Never before had he been chosen by Gayne as an opponent. He followed the older man to a corner of the yard where there was a circular area, about ten feet across, bordered by white stones set into the ground.

"This," said Gayne, "is the testing ground. We will stand, both of us, within this circle. I will attack you just as one of the evil ones might do, and try to drive you backward. You are to try to stand within the circle and, of course, to drive me out if you can. Are you ready?"

"Ready."

Hardly had the words left Lanus's lips when Gayne was upon him like a tiger. Lanus stood his ground, parrying desperately with his shield and sword. But, in spite of all he could do, he was driven backward under a rain of blows to the edge of the circle. Here he dropped to one knee to prevent his being driven farther and, using his shield and sword defensively as the older man had shown him, he managed to keep Gayne's sword from flashing through to his body. Once when Gayne was slightly off balance after one of his blows, Lanus even managed to strike out in return, and fight his way to his feet again. But a new rush by Gayne forced him again down on one knee. Finally, just as he felt he could hold out no longer, Gayne stepped backward and dropped his sword.

"All right, now let's reverse our parts. You attack, and I will be the defender."

Lanus, stung by his near defeat of a moment before, struck out vigorously, and succeeded in driving Gayne back a step or two. But beyond that, try as he might, he could make no further progress. Gayne, his eyes watchful above the edge of his shield, his sword moving quickly to parry Lanus's blows and to flick out an occasional counterstroke, blocked every assault.

At last, when Lanus was nearly worn out with his violent efforts, Gayne signaled a halt. He smiled as he saw Lanus's disappointment.

"Don't be discouraged, Lanus," he said. "That was an excellent showing. Not many soldiers of your limited experience could have held out against that attack. You show promise of becoming a fine swordsman." He sheathed his sword. "By the way," he continued as he turned toward the castle, "I think you are ready for outpost duty. You are far enough along to give a good account of yourself if an attack should come. Report to me tomorrow morning and I will start you on your duties."

And, with a final nod, Gayne left him.

7
Outpost Duty

Lanus was too excited to sleep well that night. At last he was ready for duty! He could hardly wait for morning to come so that he could begin serving his King as a full-fledged soldier. Poor Lanus! Like many another young soldier of the King, he had not yet realized that the little things he had already done—his services in garden and kitchen and hall—were just as important in the eyes of his King as the big things he hoped to do. For in the service of the King of kings, it did not matter where his duty lay; it only mattered how he performed it. But Lanus fell asleep to dream of battles and great victories, and—well, he was only human—he dreamed of himself as the hero of those wonderful scenes, cheered and applauded by Robin and Gayne and Latta and the rest.

Early the next morning, Gayne led Lanus out along a mountain path to one of the smaller outposts. Here they found a detachment of soldiers under Jon, one of the soldiers in the rescue party which had come down the mountainside on the night of Lanus's first visit to the castle.

Jon greeted Lanus warmly. "I hardly expected," he said, "when I first saw you down on the path, to serve with you on outpost duty so soon. Gayne tells me that you have learned the ways of a soldier very quickly."

Lanus flushed with pleasure. "I've done my best, sir," he said.

Gayne said, "I'll leave you with Jon and be off back to the castle. I don't need to tell you, Lanus, to do your duty. You know how important that is in the King's service."

After Gayne left, Jon showed Lanus around the outpost, which was really a self-contained little fort. It consisted of a defensive wall of earth and logs which enclosed an area in the center of the clearing. Around the inside of the wall was a ledge on which the defenders could stand to see over the top and from which they could defend the outpost. Within the enclosure was a low wooden tower from the top of which a watch was kept over the surrounding mountain slopes.

"Our job here," said Jon, "is to prevent the enemy from occupying and fortifying this area, and to keep watch for enemy activity in the woods. We take regular turns watching from the wall and from the tower. Sometimes we patrol the surrounding woodland. During the rest of the day each of us has other assigned duties. At night we return to the castle, and another group takes over.

"You will stand watch for an hour in the morning,

and an hour in the afternoon. For the rest of the time, your job will be to keep the grass cut in the clearing."

"Keep the grass cut?" asked Lanus, wondering if he had heard aright.

Jon nodded. "That is not so strange a task as you might think," he replied. "You see, if the grass outside the wall is allowed to grow long, the evil ones might creep close unobserved, and swarm over the wall in a surprise attack.

"I know," he continued with a smile, "it is not a very exciting job, but then most of our service is in the doing of regular daily tasks. It is only once in a while that the big battles occur. And the outcome of battles is usually decided on how well someone did the little jobs ahead of time."

And so Lanus found himself, on his first day of duty as a full-fledged soldier of the King, on his hands and knees in a mountain clearing, cutting grass. He was crestfallen and bewildered. Even the fact that his sword made a wonderful grass cutter, as he swung it in an arc a few inches above the ground, could not compensate for the disappointment he felt. But he swallowed his feelings and worked steadily through the long hours. The two periods of duty as watchman were welcomed breaks, but they were over only too soon, and he was back at work on the grass again.

At the end of the day, his back ached, his hand was blistered, and—less than one third of the clearing grass had been cut!

In his room at the castle that night, Lanus did some mental arithmetic. It would take three or four days at least to cut all the grass in the clearing. By that time the grass in the first section

71

would have begun to grow so that it would be nearly time to begin again. Lanus shook his head. In his mind he saw, stretching ahead, an endless succession of days of grass cutting. Was it for this he had left the valley?

Then his optimism reasserted itself. Something would happen. Perhaps there would be a battle, or perhaps he would be changed to another sort of duty. It couldn't go on forever. He climbed into bed and, this time, he fell asleep almost as soon as he touched the pillow.

But it seemed nothing would happen. Days came and went, and life at the outpost continued to be peaceful. Each sentry, ending his watch upon the tower, made the same report: "No enemy activity observed." And each sentry, as he finished his watch, went to his appointed daily task. Some strengthened the palisade wall, some felled trees at the edge of the clearing, and . . . Lanus cut grass.

Doggedly, day after day, he stuck to his task, but each day it became more tiresome and monotonous. He began to work more slowly. The old, indolent Lanus, who had been nearly smothered beneath the surface of this eager young soldier, began to assert himself again. Lanus's old nature was still with him. It wasn't that he decided to work more slowly; it was just that he wasn't quite as industrious as he had been. He got a little less of the clearing done each day, then a little less, and a little less, until he was just barely keeping the grass below the danger point.

One particularly warm afternoon when he was at the far corner of the clearing under the shadow of the trees, he stopped for a moment, to rest.

His hand was cramped and he was hot and tired. He hated to leave the cool shade of the trees and finish the part of the grass he had yet to do before evening.

"Perhaps," he thought, "if I just rest here for a minute I can do the rest of the work faster." He looked back at the outpost. The lookout could not see him here in the shadows, and no one would be likely to walk this way. Besides, it would be only for a minute. Lanus sheathed his sword and sat down in the grass. After a few seconds he leaned back until he was lying at full length. Ah, that felt better! Now just a minute's rest . . . just a minute. . . .

Lanus awoke with a start. The shadows were lengthening across the clearing, and the day was nearly over. He must have slept for two hours or more. Frantically he seized his sword and began cutting the rest of the grass. But long before he finished, the notes of the great bell from the castle signaled that the change of guard was at hand.

Now if only Jon had been at the outpost, Lanus would have gone to him at once, confessed his fault, and asked him what to do about the uncut grass. But Jon had been unexpectedly called to the castle at noon for a meeting with Latta, and the younger man who was temporarily in charge was not as well known to Lanus.

He looked at the grass he hadn't cut. It *was* rather long. Should he stay and cut it, missing his dinner thereby, or should he let it go until tomorrow? Apparently no one had noticed him sleeping. Perhaps it would be best not to raise any questions. After all, he could get here early tomorrow, and cut the remaining patch before the rest arrived. Surely, just for one night, it would be all right.

The bell sounded again, and into the clearing from the direction of the castle filed a group of soldiers. It was the night watch, ready to take over responsibility for the outpost. Lanus noticed that Robin was among them. Perhaps he should talk to Robin about the grass—but before he could act, the night watch had filed into the stockade, and the timber gate had swung shut. Slowly and with bent head, Lanus sheathed his sword and fell in line behind the rest of his watch on the path to the castle. In spite of the nap he had taken, he felt tired, and his armor weighed heavily upon him. It was not until much later that he realized that most of the load had come from the belt of truth which hung heavily about his hips.

Lanus's sleep that night was troubled. He dreamed that he was standing watch upon the castle battlement. The night was cold and un-friendly, and a dark fog shut out the stars. The wind rose to screaming pitch, and buffeted him back and forth on the top of the tower. Finally he was flung to the edge where he grabbed desper-ately at the stone, hoping to keep from being thrown to the courtyard far below. But the rough wind became the hands of the evil ones, pushing him, their voices screaming in his ears. And his sword was stuck in its sheath so that he could not draw it! Backward he was bent and out from the tower, until his fingers lost their hold on the stone and he fell downward into the fog. . . .

He awoke with Jamin's voice in his ears and Jamin's hand shaking him by the shoulder. The room was still in darkness, except for the candle which the seneschal carried. Jamin's voice was urgent.

"Get up, Lanus! Quickly! The enemy is attacking."

Lanus rolled to his feet and fumbled for his armor, blinking the sleep from his eyes.

"Wha . . . what's happened?" he managed to ask.

"The enemy has attacked and burned your post of duty on the eastern slope," said Jamin crisply. "A messenger just arrived with the news. The detachment there has fallen back and is holding a temporary defense line between the outpost and castle. Latta is leaving the castle now with reinforcements; Gayne is taking another group to reinforce the nearby outposts. You and I and a few others will stay to guard the castle."

"Jamin!"

Jamin turned in the doorway.

"Jamin, it is all my fault. I . . . I fell asleep today and didn't get all the grass cut. The enemy must have crept up through the grass to get close enough to set the stockade on fire."

Jamin came back into the room. "I'm glad you told me," he said gently. He put his hand on Lanus's shoulder. "When you know you've done wrong, and admit it, that is half the battle.

"But Lanus, when the King's soldiers are defeated as they were tonight, there is usually more than one failure involved. Only a part of the fault was yours. You see, some of the soldiers of the night detachment were not watching closely enough, or their swords would have warned them of the attackers. One of them, Wavor, had even laid his sword and shield down to relieve himself of the weight. When the attack began, he could not

find them in the darkness. As a result he was wea-
ponless, and . . . the enemy captured him."

Both men were silent for a moment, then Jamin
said briskly, "Well, we've work to do. If you are
dressed and ready, let's go." And he led the way
out of the room.

8

The Point of the Sword

The rest of that night was forever afterward a jumbled memory to Lanus. Under Jamin's direction he assisted in double barring the huge castle gates. For a while he stood guard in the gallery above the gates, then he was called by Jamin to assist in filling leather bottles with water for those fighting on the upper ridge. When the bottles were full, Lanus and another young soldier were told to carry them to the front.

"Don't fight unless you are attacked," said Jamin. "Your job is to get the water to those who need it."

The two young men set out, running swiftly along the path in the darkness. On the way they passed a number of sentries whom Latta had stationed to prevent the enemy from cutting across the path in the rear of the fighting line. But they encountered none of the evil ones. As they neared the line, an enemy lookout posted in a tall tree far to the left saw them and loosed a flaming dart. But Lanus saw it coming and, flinging up his shield, warded it off without damage.

The fighting line was quiet when the lads reached it. The soldiers, grim faced, were spread out along the edge of the clearing. Lanus was glad to see Robin among them, apparently unhurt.

"How are things going?" Lanus asked in a whisper.

"We have pushed them back into what is left of the stockade," replied Robin, also whispering. "A party is out now under Gayne trying to surround the clearing and cut them off. Then we will attack."

"You haven't been wounded, have you?" asked Lanus.

"No, I'm all right. I was off duty and resting when the enemy came in over the barricade. Before I knew it they were all around us. Del and I fought our way back to back until we reached the trees here where the rest of the detachment joined us and we stopped them."

"I wish I could stay up here with you," said Lanus, "but I must go back after more water."

Lanus made several more trips before the canteens of all the soldiers were replenished. Later, he carried a series of messages back and forth between Jamin and Latta, and several from Latta to Gayne, who was grouping his forces for an attack on the clearing from the far side. Toward morning, as Lanus was on his way up the path from the castle to the fighting line once again, he heard a shout and a clash of arms which told him that the counterattack was at last underway. He ran forward and reached the clearing while the battle was raging around the ruins of the stockade. Across the clearing toward the fighting he ran, but as he reached the spot, those of the enemy which remained broke ranks and fled across the field into the shadows of the woods. Hiding his disappointment, Lanus quietly sheathed his sword and joined in the work of clearing the wreckage from the inside of the stockade.

*   *   *

The next weeks were busy ones. The enemy, perhaps emboldened by his temporary success, was very active, and launched a series of attacks against isolated outposts and small parties traveling through the woods. The soldiers of the King rebuilt the damaged outpost and strengthened all their defensive positions. And a small group under Jon, carrying food for many days' journey, slipped away from the castle on a secret mission.

In the course of these changes, Lanus found himself assigned largely to duties in and around the castle under Jamin's supervision. He felt the change keenly, for he knew that it was due in part to his failure to do his duty at the outpost. But Lanus had learned a lesson. He would never again have to be told to do his best at whatever he was given to do. Therefore, each time that Jamin assigned him a task, whether it was picking beans in the garden or carrying boxes in or out of the castle storerooms, Lanus did it as thoroughly as though his life depended on it. And he learned a great truth—that if you try to do each job as well as you can, that job becomes interesting, even though it was dull before, and thus joy may be found even in unpleasant tasks.

Jamin noted Lanus's changed attitude with approval and, as the weeks went by, gave him more and more responsibility. Lanus on his part learned to admire Jamin for his careful planning and orderly thinking. And he tried to be like him.

All of this, of course, meant that Lanus had little opportunity to join in the skirmishes which occurred outside the castle, though he still attended the daily sword drills in the castle yard. Only twice was he called on to join rescue parties which sallied from the castle to the aid of hard-pressed groups of soldiers.

On one of these occasions he had his first actual fight with one of the enemy. It was at night on the path below the castle. Two of the King's soldiers had been attacked by several of the enemy, and the rescue party had arrived just in time to prevent them from being overcome. Lanus found himself faced by one of the evil ones, a large, ferocious creature with a huge sword. But the lessons he had learned from Gayne stood him in good stead, and Lanus was able to beat off his attacks. For several minutes they stood toe to toe, exchanging blows. Then the evil one, glancing over his shoulder, saw that his comrades were being driven from the field. After a last murderous thrust at Lanus, he broke away and disappeared into the woods. But though Lanus had won no victory, he was satisfied to realize that he had acquitted himself well, and had turned every blow aimed at him by the enemy. And he was pleased to find that, after that encounter, his shield of faith had taken on a slightly brighter luster.

Jamin was almost as pleased when Lanus told

him about it, and he clapped Lanus heartily on the back. "That is a fine beginning, lad," he said. "Don't worry about winning great victories. For victories are just the result of aiming each blow well."

Lanus grinned and began nailing a lid on a box of dried fruit. "My great victory will be long in coming then," he said, "for I was able to strike only a few blows.

"But do you know, Jamin," he continued seriously, "my sword was light as a feather, and seemed to guide itself."

"That is a good sign," said Jamin. "That only happens when the soldier's arm is practiced and his heart ready for the battle, and when he seeks only the King's glory, not his own."

Jamin sat quietly for a moment, watching with thoughtful eyes the swing of Lanus's broad shoulders as he drove the nails home. Then he asked, "How much time at sword practice does Gayne give you each afternoon?"

Lanus laid down his hammer to get another strip of wood for the box. "About an hour. Part of the time he instructs, and for the rest, I fence with Robin or one of the other men. Gayne has been so busy at the outposts lately that his time with us has been limited."

Jamin nodded. "I am too busy in the castle to get out to sword practice in the afternoons," he said. "Usually Latta and I practice together in the mornings, but lately he too has been spending nearly all his time in the field. Would you like to spend half an hour at sword practice with me tomorrow morning?"

Would he? Lanus's eyes sparkled and he accepted promptly. For among the young soldiers it was understood that Jamin, short and round though he was, was an outstanding swordsman. Some said that he was even better than Latta, but this was disputed. At any rate, Jamin was such a busy person that few of the young men had had opportunity to cross swords with him.

Early the next morning Jamin and Lanus went to a quiet spot in the castle garden, adjusted their helmets and shields, and began sword practice. But Lanus soon found that Jamin's swordplay was not at all the same as Gayne's. For Jamin, while lacking Gayne's powerful sweeping strokes, handled his sword with incredible speed. He used the point as well as the edge, and his swordpoint seemed to be everywhere. In one instant it threatened Lanus's face; in the next, it flicked past the edge of his shield to prick unerringly at a joint in his armor. At the same time, Jamin easily warded off Lanus's counterblows.

At the end of thirty minutes, Lanus was exhausted and thoroughly beaten. Jamin lowered his sword and stepped back. "I think we've both had enough for this time," he smiled.

Lanus sheathed his sword ruefully. "I thought I had begun to learn how to use the sword," he said, "but now I find that I know very little about it."

Jamin nodded seriously. "No one really knows the sword, Lanus. It is greater than any of us, though it was made for our use. The more we practice with it, the more we find there is to learn."

"Tell me, Jamin," asked Lanus, "why it is that your style of swordplay differs so much from Gayne's? Gayne teaches us to use the edge of the sword, while you use more often the point."

"Both edge and point have value," said Jamin as they began to walk toward the castle. "Gayne and Latta are both tall, powerful men and they love to use the sword in broad, sweeping strokes. Because I have less reach and stature, I practiced the use of the point as well as the blade. As the great soldier Paul once said, *'Every man hath his proper gift of God, one after this manner, and another after that.'*

"I sometimes think, though," he continued reflectively, "that Latta and Gayne lean too much to the use of the edge. Great men of old like Peter and Paul won great victories with the edge of the sword, but it is sometimes forgotten that they used the sharp point as well. The sword, after all, is an instrument of great delicacy. It can pierce through the heart as easily as it can slash through the armor of ignorance and unbelief. And in this present day, when so much of our combat is in individual encounters in the close spaces of the woods, where branches and vines obstruct the strokes, I think the point of the sword is often better. Yet there are few who learn to use it well."

"I should like to learn the use of the point," said Lanus.

"I will teach you," nodded Jamin approvingly. "I have been watching your movements as you work about the castle. You have the stature and reach to use the edge, and you also have balance and flexibility, which are needed to use the fine point of the sword. If you practice both, you may one day be a better swordsman than I, or Gayne, or perhaps even Latta—who knows?"

And so, morning after morning, Lanus practiced with Jamin the use of the swordpoint. His progress was slow, for the art was difficult and required much study and practice. But gradually, bit by bit, he learned. Each morning, under Jamin's skillful teaching, some new twist or thrust or movement was learned, and those already mastered were practiced, until finally the sword began to move easily, naturally, like an extension of his own arm. Try as he might, however, he could not best Jamin, whose sword seemed at times like a ray of light, flicking out from behind his shield.

But Lanus did find that his morning lessons with Jamin helped him a great deal in the afternoon sword drill which Gayne conducted. Many of the young soldiers, who before could defeat him with ease, found themselves bewildered by this new Lanus, whose swordpoint flashed past their guards in telling thrusts. He could now cross swords with Robin on even terms, much to the delight of that young man, whose dearest wish was to see Lanus advance in the service of the King.

Once Lanus even slid his sword past Gayne's guard and, had Gayne not nimbly twisted aside, would have touched him through the center joints of his armor.

After the bout, Gayne asked sharply, "Has Jamin been instructing you?" and when Lanus nodded, he said, "I thought so. That thrust was like him. Well, there is no finer swordsman in the castle than Jamin, though his method is somewhat different from my own. Learn what you can from him, for it will do you no harm."

9
The Cleft of the Rock

It was shortly after this that Jamin stepped up the morning practice sessions from half an hour to an hour in length. When Lanus questioned him, he only said, "More practice will help both of us. We may be needing our swords one of these days."

Then Jon and his men appeared at the castle gate one evening, tired, dusty, and worn, and Jon was closeted for many hours with Gayne, Latta, and Jamin.

The next day Latta ordered an assemblage in the great castle hall. All of the men and women of the castle, except those on necessary duties, were present. Latta, a tall, striking figure with the lamplight gleaming from his silver hair and armor, rose to speak.

"Soldiers of the King," he said, "there is a difficult and dangerous mission which must be accomplished in the King's service. Only a few of you can go, and they will be chosen from among those who volunteer."

He paused for breath, and as he did so, there was a great jingle of harness and armor as every soldier in the room rose to his feet. Lanus rose with the rest, though he had no hope of being chosen. Latta looked about him and smiled.

"Be seated," he said. "I see that we will have no trouble finding volunteers, even before you know what you will be called on to do.

"The mission concerns our brother Wavor, who was captured, you remember, when the enemy overran the outpost some weeks ago. A rescue party was sent out, led by Jon, which followed the raiders down the mountain chain and attacked them twice trying to break through to Wavor to free him. The enemy cordon was too strong and they could not pierce it, though they did get close enough to see him. Wavor was held, with his hands bound and his eyes blindfolded, in the center of a group of evil ones. He was without his sword and shield, so he has little chance of escaping.

"Jon and his party followed until the raiders reached Castle Despair, which lies far to the south in the mountain chain. Into this castle Wavor was taken, and is no doubt held in one of the dungeons there.

"One of our number has volunteered to lead a rescue attempt against the castle itself. He is, I believe, more qualified than anyone else to do so. I will let him select his own assistants from this host of volunteers."

Latta sat down. Then, to Lanus's great surprise, Jamin slowly rose from his seat at Latta's side and faced the assembly.

"This is not a mission for many," he said, looking from face to face around the gathering, 'For there is no restraint to the Lord to save by many or by few.' Therefore, I will take only two men with me. Both are young men, but I feel that they have the qualities which this mission requires. I choose Robin . . . and Lanus!"

Lanus was completely dazed with surprise and happiness. He had been chosen! He hardly noticed when Jamin finished his brief speech and sat down, or when, a short time later, Latta signaled that the meeting was at an end. Not until several of the young soldiers who had been sitting near crowded around to congratulate him did he begin to get his wits about him. Then he felt a hearty clap on the shoulder, and there was Robin, grinning happily.

"Did you hear him, Lanus? We're going—both of us!"

"Yes," said Lanus, finding his voice again, "let's find Jamin and ask when we start."

Jamin was still at the head of the hall, talking with Latta and Gayne. The two young soldiers hung back respectfully, waiting to be recognized. Then Latta saw them and waved them to approach.

"Here are your two helpers, Jamin," he said, putting a hand on each of the young men's shoulders. "Robin, you have proven yourself many times over to be a good soldier. And Lanus, Jamin tells me you are fast becoming one of our better swordsmen. I am sure you both will serve your King well on this difficult mission."

Jamin said, "Lads, we will leave the castle tomorrow morning. Get your arms and armor ready. Lanus, see that food is prepared to take along.

Robin, get Wavor's sword and shield, which were left behind when he was captured. We will take them with us in addition to our own. Both of you come to my room this evening after dinner and we will lay our plans."

An hour before daybreak the following morning, the castle gate swung silently open and three soldiers moved out onto the mountain ridge. In single file they headed southward down the mountain chain, Jamin, the leader, holding his sword high to light the way, for it was still dark. Sunup found them several miles from the castle and still moving steadily southward. All that day the three pressed on through the thick woodland which covered the mountain slopes, pausing only to eat, and keeping constant watch for enemy scouts.

"Though," remarked Jamin, "they are creatures of the night, and are not frequently to be found in the sunshine."

As evening drew near, they approached a rocky peak which projected skyward from the backbone of the mountain ridge. Toward this Jamin led them and, just as the sun went down, they clambered up its slopes. Near the top was a cleft in the rock, and into it Jamin led the way. There the three soldiers found themselves in a dry, comfortable cave, from the mouth of which could be seen, far below, the rolling wooded ridges of the great mountains.

"How did you ever come to find such a hiding place as this?" asked Robin with interest, turning from the view.

Jamin smiled. "This cave," he said, "has been known to the soldiers of the King for generations. It was used by the great warrior David, who found here a safe retreat from his enemies. And since his time it has been used by many another. Look!"

Jamin drew his sword, and held it high, so that it illuminated the far wall of the cave. There, cut into the stone face were the words: *"Lead me to the rock that is higher than I. For Thou hast been a shelter for me, and a strong tower from the enemy."*

"David cut those words," said Jamin, "and many a hard-pressed soldier, hiding here from his enemies, has been thankful for them.

"We need keep no lookout tonight," he continued, "for no evil thing ever scales this rock nor comes near this cleft."

Jamin fastened his sword to a projection in the rock so that it lit the interior of the cave. By its light, the three men sat down and made a hearty meal of the food they had brought with them. Afterward Jamin showed them a small pool of fresh water at the back of the cave, at which they drank and filled their water bottles.

"There is a hollow in the top of the rock," explained Jamin in answer to a question from Lanus, "which catches the water from heaven and sends it down through openings in the rock to this pool."

The night had become chilly, and Jamin fastened his cloak across the narrow entrance of the cave to form a door.

"Let me go down the slope and gather wood for a fire," suggested Lanus, but Jamin shook his head.

"There is a better way to warm yourself," he said. "Draw your swords and lay the blades across your breasts."

Robin and Lanus did so, wondering, and found to their surprise that their bodies became warm.

"The sword of the spirit will keep you warmer than any fire made with the sticks of this world," said Jamin. "Many a night have I spent alone on mountaintops with only my sword to warm me, and I never wanted for heat." He was silent for a few moments. "And how many soldiers there are," he continued in a lower tone, "who never realize all the wonders and uses of the sword, and who draw it only in battle.

"But let me show you something else." He took his sword from the rock where he had fastened it, and laid it on the ground it front of him. "Now, cross your swords over mine," he said, and when the three swords lay crossed on the ground, the cave was not only completely lit with a soft glow, but became also comfortably warm.

The other two looked at each other in astonishment. "This is wonderful!" Lanus burst out.

"So it is," echoed Robin. "What causes it, Jamin?"

"When two or three of the King's followers lay their swords together, the light and warmth is increased many times. The sword was so designed by the King, for He wants His soldiers to remember that they must work and fellowship together. 'Forsake not the assembling of yourselves together,' He once said. If we could live without each other, we might allow anger to separate us, and our brotherhood be destroyed, but the King has not willed it so."

"The sword of the spirit . . ." said Lanus thoughtfully. "It defends us, it lights our way, it pierces through armor, it warms us, and it draws us together in fellowship. Are there other things that we have yet to learn about this wonderful sword?"

"There are others," said Jamin. "Perhaps you will

94

learn some of them before this mission is over."

"There is a thing that I have heard about the sword," said Robin. "That is, that it sometimes shines with a brilliance brighter than that of the sun itself. I asked Jon about it, and he had heard of it too, but had never seen it."

Jamin leaned back comfortably on one elbow, and fixed his eyes on the three swords crossed before him.

"It has happened," he said quietly. "If you like, I will tell you of it before we sleep tonight."

*   *   *

"You have read in the King's book," began Jamin, "of how the King came to the valley long ago as a poor carpenter and went about doing good, and of how men rejected Him.

"But there was a fight fought by the King while He was here of which you may not have read. This was a duel between the King and the great Evil One himself, and it happened when the King first came to the valley.

"You remember the King had sent word by His messengers that He would come to the valley some day. The great Evil One heard of that message, and had prepared several deadly weapons with which to attack Him. When the King came, He spent forty days alone here on the mountain slopes preparing Himself for His mission in the valley. And the master of evil came to the mountain to find Him.

"'This is my valley,' said the Evil One, 'I have taken it from you by my cleverness, and I plan to keep it mine. If you would enter the valley, you must first defeat me in single combat!'

"The King had no weapons save those which His

95

soldiers carry, but the Evil One brought with him the best of the evil armory. He carried the flaming dart of hunger, the sharp spear of pride, and the heavy battleax of lust. And he brought, also, a two-edged sword. This sword was a copy of the King's own weapon, except that it had the saw-toothed edges of deceit.

"You may read of that battle if you like. The Evil One attacked with each of his weapons in turn, but the King, standing steadily as a rock, turned each blow aside with His sword and shield. And the King's sword was that day a shining sword, a flame of fire against which the weapons of the Evil One clashed but could not win. Even the sword of the Evil One—the sword so carefully forged in the armory of evil—was turned aside. The Evil one fought with all his skill, but the shining sword forced him backward along the mountain crest and down the slope toward the valley.

"Not until the Evil One was beaten did the King lower His sword. 'Get thee hence!' He said, and the master of evil, hearing his own doom in that voice, slunk away. Many times afterward did the Evil One seek to destroy the King by trickery, deceit, and force, but never again did he dare to face Him alone.

"Often while He was here in the valley did the King use the sword against some evil thing, and each time its blade shone in His hand with a brilliance like the sun's. Since He left, the sword has shone less frequently.

"It shone in soldier Peter's hand on the day of Pentecost when he first drew it after the King's departure. It shone in the hand of Paul on many occasions when he fought for his King against the forces of ignorance and superstition. And it has shone at different times through the years when drawn by the great warriors whom the King has raised up in times of crises. Sometimes, too, the sword has shone unexpectedly when drawn by some unknown and humble soldier in defense of his King.

"These shinings of the sword have seldom come more than once in a single generation. But whenever the sword has shone, it has been the signal for a great victory over the forces of evil. In my lifetime, no sword has shone, for this seems to be a day of difficult battles and small victories. Perhaps, who knows, the next shining of the sword may be when the King comes again to muster us into His eternal army. May that time be soon. . . .

"And now it is late and we have many miles to travel tomorrow. Let us sleep."

10

Valley of Despair

Early the next morning, Jamin awakened his two companions. The three soldiers stood together at the mouth of the cave, while Jamin sounded the morning trumpet call, asking the King for guidance in the day ahead. After a hasty breakfast, they left the cave and, descending to the forest, continued south along the mountain ridge.

As they went, Lanus noticed that the forest became thicker and gloomier, with high trees meeting far overhead to shut out the sunlight. The danger of attack was much greater here in the shadows, and the three soldiers carried their swords in their hands and their shields slung ready for use. All that day they traveled with hardly a pause, and that night they camped in the woods on a small knoll where, under Jamin's direction, they piled rocks into a defensive wall around them. Each of the three took turns watching while the other two slept, for they were getting deep into enemy territory.

Lanus had the middle watch and, when Jamin shook him awake, the night was cold and dark. After Jamin had gone to sleep, wrapped in his traveling cloak and with the heat-giving sword lying on his breast, Lanus sat cross-legged, staring out into the darkness. The light from his sword shone on the tree trunks around and down the dark avenues between the trees. Lanus was glad that this light was of such a nature that evil ones could not see it, for its glow would have invited attack. Twice in the distance as the night wore on, Lanus heard the high-pitched wind-wail, which told that the enemy was abroad in strength, and once the sword light flared up strongly, indicating that some of the evil ones were nearby. But if they knew of the presence of the little band, they gave no sign. Finally the moon peeped briefly through the clouds, and Lanus saw by its position that it was time to call Robin to take over the watch. Soon afterward Lanus was sound asleep, to awaken in the gray dawn only when Robin shook him.

"Today," said Jamin, as they were eating breakfast, "we will reach the castle."

"And what do we do then?" asked Lanus.

Jamin only smiled. "Let's take one thing at a time," he said. "Our first problems are the miles which lie between us and the castle."

They set out again, moving southward and ever deeper into the forest. The sky, gray in the morning, grew darker as they advanced, and wisps of fog began to drift across their path.

"Perhaps it will storm," said Robin.

"No," said Jamin over his shoulder, "near the

castle of despair it is always dark. Stay close and keep your weapons ready."

After several more hours of steady travel, during which it grew still darker, Jamin suddenly halted. Motioning for silence, he pointed ahead to where a deep gorge cut across the mountain ridge. Then he led the way cautiously forward to the edge of the gorge and, parting the underbrush carefully with his hands, pointed downward. Lanus caught his breath. From their feet the ground fell away in a precipice to a narrow valley far below. And rising from the bottom of the gorge, partially shrouded in an oppressive black fog, were the towers of a great stone castle. This, Lanus realized, was the castle of despair.

The castle was black, like the fog, and appeared cold and brooding and sinister, like some evil beast that crouched in the valley, waiting to spring upon its victim. There were no lights nor signs of life. Around the castle was a still, black lake, reaching nearly from side to side of the narrow valley. A stone causeway led across this lake to the castle gates.

Jamin turned and led the way back several hundred yards to where a large boulder thrust itself out of the ridge. Here the three seated themselves on the ground. "We will eat now, for we will need all our strength for what lies ahead," said Jamin in guarded tones.

As they ate, Jamin explained his plan. "The main castle gate," he said, "is well guarded. However, there is a small side door to the castle of despair which few know about. It is reached by crossing the causeway, then skirting the outside of the wall. Usually there is only a single guard on this door. If we overpower him, we can get into the castle. Once inside, I know the way through back passages to the dungeon where Wavor must be. We must release him and give him the sword and shield which we brought for him; then we must fight our way out."

Lanus, who had been listening intently, looked up with a puzzled frown. "But you haven't told us how you plan to unlock the door to the castle, or how you will open the dungeon door to get Wavor out!"

Jamin smiled. "Did I not tell you that you would learn more about the wonders of the sword of the spirit before this mission is accomplished? Draw your swords. Do you see the five grooves that run the length of the blade?"

Both lads nodded, and Robin said, "I've often wondered what they were."

"The sword," said Jamin, "is the master key to all the locks in the castles of the enemy. It was so designed by our Lord and King, who knew all there is to know about locks long before the great Evil One built the first of his castles. The enemy cannot make a lock that this key will not open, and that is one of his greatest weaknesses."

Jamin continued, "But there is another serious problem in our path. And I think from his expression Robin was going to ask about it."

Robin nodded. "I was wondering how we are to get across the causeway without the alarm being raised."

"That will be difficult," said Jamin. "But I have thought of a way. You have noticed the black fog which hangs about the castle. It is an evil fog which is called 'the blackness of darkness' or 'the blackness of despair,' and was created by the great Evil One himself as a defense for the castle.

It is a poisonous vapor which robs those who breathe it of their strength. But having created it, the enemy cannot entirely control it, and the book of the King tells us that the Evil One himself will be overcome by it at last!

"It has this advantage for us. The evil ones, whose eyes can penetrate ordinary darkness, cannot see clearly through this fog. Therefore, we may be able to use the blackness of darkness to conceal us. If we wait on the valley slopes until the fog eddies across the causeway, hiding it from the view of the guards on the gate, we can cross without being seen.

"There is a principle there," continued Jamin, "to which soldiers of the King might well take heed. The enemy's greatest strength is often his weakness, and the very excess of evil may provide the avenue through which salvation will come."

"But if we breathe the fog, will we not lose our strength?" asked Robin.

Again Jamin's face broke into a smile, and his eyes twinkled. "Your swords again, gentlemen," he said, "your wonderful swords. Hold the flat of the blade a few inches in front of your noses and mouths, and any air you take in will be purified and sweetened!"

He stood up as if to go, and Lanus, who had been listening silently, said, "Tell us, Jamin, how is it that you know so much about the castle and the habits of the enemy?"

Jamin, his face once again serious, replied, "It is because once, many years ago, I too was a captive of the enemy, and was held in the dungeon of this very castle. But that is a long story that I must tell you another time."

From his breast he drew forth the silver trumpet.

Then noting the look of surprise on Lanus's face, he smiled.

"It is perfectly safe, Lanus," he said. "Have you forgotten that the ears of the evil ones are deaf to the notes of the trumpet, just as their eyes are blind to the swordlight? But this call will be heard by our Lord and King, whom we trust for strength and guidance."

Raising the trumpet to his lips, Jamin blew a beautiful, clear note which echoed across the mountains. Then, turning to the other two, he continued, "Never neglect the silver trumpet, lads. Use it often while on the King's business. And if ever all seems lost, sound an urgent call for help upon it, for so has many a despairing soldier been saved. And now, we must go."

He drew his sword. Robin and Lanus crossed theirs upon it, and the three comrades stood silent for a moment, while the glow from the crossed swords lit up the gloom around them and the warmth of fellowship penetrated their bodies. Then Jamin turned and led the way toward the valley of despair.

The three moved quietly along the edge of the precipice until they came to a small ravine thickly grown with underbrush, which led steeply down into the main gorge. Down this ravine they crept until they reached a point only a few feet from the valley floor. Here, hidden by the underbrush, they crouched, watching the slow eddying movements of the deadly fog which hung in strips like tattered curtains around the castle walls.

For hours they waited. The gloom of the valley was so intense that they had no idea whether it was noon or evening. From inside the castle they heard an occasional low and far-off cry, like a creature in agony, but, except for that, the whole valley seemed long dead and deserted.

Finally a patch of fog drifted in front of the castle gate, then another. The two together grew in size, slowly, steadily, until nearly the whole causeway was swathed in blackness. Jamin rose silently. The time had come! With drawn sword he led the way out of the ravine and along the edge of the lake to the causeway. Then, in close single file, each with his hand on the shoulder of the one ahead, the three moved slowly out on the black stones. As they entered the fog, they held their swords vertically in front of their mouths and found, as Jamin had predicted, that the air they breathed remained clear and sweet.

The causeway was wide enough for two to have walked abreast, but the stones were black and slippery, and even with the help of the light cast by the sword it was difficult to determine where the edge was, for the swordlight penetrated the fog for only a short distance. Cautiously, step by step, the three moved forward. After what seemed like an hour (though it was only a few minutes) Jamin stopped. Lanus, looking past him, saw just ahead the iron-bound gates of the castle stretching upward into the fog.

Jamin turned sharply to the left and led the way along a narrow ledge at the base of the castle wall. After a short distance, the ledge broadened and Jamin slowed his pace. Then suddenly they broke out of the fog. There, not ten feet away, was a small archway in the castle wall. And, standing at its entrance, with sword drawn and teeth bared in a snarl, was one of the evil ones!

He had evidently heard their footsteps, for he was bending forward peering intently into the fog. When he saw them, he straightened and opened his mouth to shout. At the same instant, Jamin leaped forward like a tiger unleashed and, with a tremendous slashing blow of his sword, silenced him before he could utter a sound. As the guard's body slumped to the ground, Jamin turned quickly and whispered: "Robin, stay here and guard the entrance. Keep it clear at all costs, for it is the only way we can get out again. Lanus, unlock the door."

While Jamin wiped the blade of his sword, Lanus stepped into the archway, where he found his way blocked by a heavy stone door. Carefully he fitted the blade of his sword into the keyhole, pushed until the entire blade had disappeared inside, then twisted gently. There was a click and the door swung easily open. Jamin, who had come up behind Lanus, went in first, with his blade ready. Lanus pulled his sword free and followed.

They found themselves in a dark, stone-floored corridor. Jamin led the way confidently through a maze of turns and twists, and down several flights of steps until they reached a level where the floors were damp and slippery, and water dripped continuously from the walls. Finally he stopped in front of a large iron door.

"Keep watch," he whispered to Lanus. He bent and slid his sword into the keyhole. A moment later, with a loud, creaking sound, the door swung back. Jamin, holding his sword high, slipped inside, leaving Lanus alone in the corridor. A moment later Jamin emerged again, his face shining with joy. Leaning on his arm, weak and pale but smiling, was Wavor!

11

The Battle of the Causeway

Jamin lowered Wavor to a sitting position against the wall of the passage, gave him a drink of water from the bottle slung at his belt, and made him eat some food from his pouch. After a few mouthfuls the color came back again to Wavor's face. While he was eating, Lanus stepped to the door of the dungeon and looked inside. It was a damp, windowless room, the floor of which was mud and water. In a small niche in the wall, a single candle was burning, and by its light could be read the words, *"Your King has forgotten you,"* cut into the stone of the wall. Other than a small wooden bench and table, there was no furniture. Lanus turned away with a shudder.

Outside in the corridor, he found Wavor on his feet, weak, but ready to go. He was still wearing his helmet, breastplate, belt, and shoes. (Lanus learned later that the enemy had been unable to solve the secret fastenings which held them on.) Jamin now handed him the shield and sword, which he had left on the field of battle on the night of his capture. Wavor's eyes lit with joy when he saw his weapons, and, as he grasped the sword, he seemed nearly his old self once again.

"We must hurry," whispered Jamin, leading the way back along the passage toward the stairway. Wavor followed and Lanus brought up the rear. As they turned the corner, Lanus heard, far down the corridor behind him, the high wailing of the enemy's war cry, and knew that they had been seen. Jamin heard, too, and increased his speed up the steep flight of steps. Lanus held his sword behind him as he ran and, when the light flared high, knew that the enemy was close. Near the top of the steps he turned. There, running swiftly upward toward him in the circle of light cast by the sword, were three of the enemy, large, snarling, and terrible.

Lanus stopped. On the narrow steps they would have to come at him one at a time. He had barely time to set himself before the first of the enemy was upon him, swinging a black sword in a powerful overhand blow at his head!

In the battle on the stairs, Lanus's long hours of training under Jamin in the use of the point stood him in good stead, for there was no room to cut. Lanus flung up his shield to ward off the blow, and at the same time thrust his own sword straight forward at the enemy's exposed chest. The enemy's blow, falling on his shield, staggered him by its force, but he felt his own blade go home. Backward down the steps the evil one toppled into the arms of his comrades. The first bout was won.

The second creature attacked more cautiously and with the sword point, thrusting at Lanus from behind a black shield. But Lanus's sword, feeling light as a feather and moving almost of its own will, parried his thrusts, and then lashed out in its turn, forcing him to give ground down the stairway. Lanus followed him down, feinted a thrust at his face, and then, with a beautiful twist of the wrist that Jamin had taught him, drove the sword home past his shield.

Two were down—and the third one turned and fled. Just then Jamin and Wavor, who had come back looking for Lanus, appeared at the top of the steps. Lanus bounded up to join them, and Jamin again led the way toward the side door, and freedom. The castle was aroused now, and the wailing of the enemy echoed down all of the dark corridors. Twice, groups of the evil ones went by as they crouched hidden in side passages, but finally, without further encounters, they managed to reach the stone door.

Outside under the archway stood Robin, and at his feet lay the still forms of not one but three of the enemy.

"I've been pretty busy," smiled Robin. "Fortunately they came one at a time!"

Jamin quickly locked the door from the outside to stop pursuit, then turned to lead the way back along the ledge.

But the fog had lifted.

Through the gloom of the valley, Lanus could see the castle gates standing open and several of the enemy on the causeway. Quickly Jamin drew the King's soldiers together on the ledge for a whispered council of war. As yet they had not been seen, but they might be at any moment.

"We must rush the causeway," said Jamin. "Robin and Lanus will lead the way and clear the causeway of those who are on it. I will, in the meantime, try to stop the attack of those who will come out the gate. Wavor is in no condition to fight yet, and will stay in the middle of the group."

The four soldiers touched their swords together briefly, then Robin and Lanus moved silently to the front. It was the first time the two friends had fought side by side, and Robin flashed Lanus a warm smile as they moved out along the ledge. Quietly and swiftly, with swords ready, the little group advanced. But while they were still some yards away from the causeway, one of the evil ones saw them, and raised a cry of alarm. In the same instant, Jamin's trumpet blast rang out, and the King's men went forward with a spirited rush that carried them on to the causeway. There Robin and Lanus turned shoreward and, side by side, drove against the four evil ones which remained on the causeway. Robin's sword was steady and sure, as he parried, cut, and parried again, his powerful strokes shearing off chips of shield and armor. Lanus used both the edge and the point as Jamin had taught him, throwing the length of his body into his thrusts. The enemy, taken by surprise, gave ground rapidly at first, but soon rallied and began fighting back fiercely. Mustering all their skill, the two young soldiers inched forward.

On the narrow causeway only two of the enemy could attack at once. Nevertheless, this was the hardest fighting Lanus had yet encountered, for these were apparently some of the enemy's better swordsmen. He threw a sidelong glance at Robin who, with his steady but not brilliant style, was pressing his man backward, though his

112

clenched teeth showed the effort it cost him.

"I'm doing as well as Robin," thought Lanus, "even a little better!" The thought gave him a thrill of pleasure, and he pressed forward with a furious attack against the huge creature facing him. If only he could force the evil one off balance, perhaps he could push him into the lake and reduce the odds to three against two.

Suddenly Lanus saw an opening in the enemy's guard. He leaped forward, his whole body extended in a sudden thrust. Then, too late, he saw the trap. Leering triumphantly, the evil one twisted aside! Viciously he swung his black sword in a whistling arc! Lanus threw up his left arm, desperately. He felt the blow strike solidly against his shield of faith, then, clawing and off balance, he hurtled over the edge of the causeway and into the black water below!

Weighted and sinking, struggling in the blackness, Lanus heard, faint and far away, the voice of Jamin. "Your sword, Lanus! Hold onto your sword!"

Lanus had not lost his grip on the sword. Now, in obedience to the voice, but more by instinct than design, he grasped the blade with his free hand. To his surprise the movement pulled his head above water. The sword, floating on the surface, held him up! Quickly he hooked both elbows over the blade, so that it lay across his chest supporting the upper part of his body. Then he shook the water from his eyes.

Above him on the causeway, the light of Robin's sword still glowed, as he struggled against two of the enemy. Robin was on the defensive now, fighting desperately to keep himself from being driven back against Jamin at the castle end of the causeway. Jamin, on his part, was too busy with the horde of evil ones who were crowding out of the castle gate to turn and help him. Lanus groaned. There was no hope now—and it was all his fault. If he had not tried to outdo Robin . . .

Then he remembered the silver trumpet, and the words of Jamin concerning it: "If ever all seems lost, sound an urgent call for help upon it, for so has many a despairing soldier been saved." Hastily Lanus groped below the surface for his trumpet. Shaking the water from it, he put it to his lips and blew with all his might. All of his despair and regret for his failure did Lanus put into that trumpet call. And as the notes died away, an idea came to him.

Perhaps he could still help. If he could swim strongly enough to reach the causeway *behind* the evil ones who were attacking Robin, he might turn the tide. Maybe, after all, his fall was not entirely wasted! He threw a hasty glance at the causeway to make sure none of the enemy was watching him. Then he kicked out as hard as he could.

It was slow going, for his plunge had carried him some distance from the causeway, but bit by bit Lanus made progress. He slanted his course so as to reach the causeway well shoreward of the battle, hoping fervently that none of the evil ones would catch sight of him. Finally his outstretched hand touched the stone and, with a final effort, he pulled himself out of the water onto the causeway. He was still breathless from his struggles in the water but there was no time to rest. Already Robin was being driven back. Lanus scrambled to his feet and raced along the causeway, sword in hand and feet slapping soggily against the wet stone. He must be in time—he must!

One of the four evil ones attacking Robin heard him and spun around. But before he could set himself, a slashing blow from Lanus's sword rang squarely on his shield and toppled him into the lake. A second blow caught another of the enemy in the act of turning and sent him sprawling to the causeway. At the same instant Robin, taking advantage of the confusion occasioned by Lanus's sudden appearance, sent his sword flashing past the shield of his opponent in a fatal thrust. As the evil one slumped to the stone, the last of the four—the one who had been responsible for sending Lanus into the lake—leaped into the dark water and, in spite of his armor's weight, swam strongly off toward the castle. The causeway was won!

Lanus's rush carried him past Robin to where Jamin was fighting. There, his short legs planted firmly, his sword moving more rapidly than Lanus had ever seen it, Jamin was holding the causeway alone against terrible odds. While only two of the evil ones who crowded out of the castle gate could attack him at once, the eager, enemy-fighting men were changing places so that those facing Jamin were always fresh and strong. But the King's soldier, his eyes sparkling and a half smile on his lips, was standing like a rock. Parrying, slashing, thrusting, his sword seemed to multiply itself into a dozen blades, flashing in the valley gloom. Behind him, whitefaced and trembling, too weak to join in the fighting, stood Wavor, his upraised shield protecting Jamin's head against the fiery darts which were raining down from the wall.

Without stopping to draw breath, Lanus threw

himself into the fight at Jamin's side. Robin, turning from his fallen foe, found that there was no room for him to fight beside the other two, and raised his shield with Wavor's to form a protective covering over them. Jamin threw a hasty glance over his shoulder.

"The way is clear," he said. "Good. Let us give ground slowly."

At a signal from Jamin, the King's men moved backward along the causeway toward the shore. When they neared the land and were well out of range of darts from the wall, Jamin called over his shoulder, "Robin, we can hold them here for a while. Help Wavor to the top of the ravine and wait for us there."

When the other two had gone, Jamin and Lanus set themselves to the task of turning back the successive enemy rushes. Lanus had by this time caught his second wind and was breathing more easily. He found himself engaged once again with the huge creature who earlier had dumped him into the lake. This monster pushed his way forward, raining blows upon Lanus's shield almost as Gayne had done. But Lanus, fighting coolly and carefully, found that Jamin's training was adequate and, with the plunging point of the sword, forced his adversary to give ground.

After a while a low whistle sounded from the top of the hill and, throwing a quick glance over his shoulder, Lanus saw the glow of Robin's sword upon the summit. Jamin nodded once, and the two soldiers broke away from the fight and ran across the valley floor to the mouth of the ravine. Here, where steep rocky walls protected their flanks, they turned again to beat off their pursuers. Then, step by step, fighting all the way, they

116

backed up the ravine toward the summit.

In the narrow ravine, Lanus found the same adversary again and again in the forefront of the attack, swinging powerful blows which rang against the shield of faith. Finally, mustering all his skill, Lanus drove his point under the enemy's guard, wounding him. With a final snarl, the evil one dropped back and away, and his place was taken by another.

The last few feet of the ravine were very steep. But at the top stood Robin with a hand outstretched and, grasping it, first Lanus and then Jamin were hauled to safety. Then Robin stepped in to bear his share of the fighting, driving back from the crest each futile, scrambling advance of the enemy, while the others rested. Between these attacks, Jamin unfolded in whispers the rest of his plan.

"Here we must split forces again," he said. "Wavor cannot travel fast, and must be given a start. Two of us will stay here and hold the top of the ravine while the third, with Wavor, starts back up the ridge. There are other ways by which the evil ones can reach the top of the precipice, but they are far down the gorge, so we are safe here for an hour or more. However, those who stay must slip away at the first opportunity."

Robin said with a smile, "Lanus and I are the youngest and have the longest legs, sir. And we are both good runners. Let us stay behind."

Jamin smiled in his turn. "I'm afraid logic is on your side," he said. "I would like to stay myself, but," he looked down at his round body, "this is a job you can do better than I."

He helped the resting Wavor to his feet, and together they moved off up the ridge, the glow from Jamin's sword lighting the forest around. Left alone, Robin and Lanus devoted themselves to keeping the enemy from climbing the ravine to the top. For more than half an hour the attacks continued, then they slackened and ceased. By the light of their swords, the lads saw the last of the evil ones retreating out of sight down the ravine, apparently to plan some new attack.

For only a few moments longer they waited, to make certain that no more immediate attacks would come. Then they quietly stole away from the crest and, with Robin setting the pace, went off up the ridge after Jamin. After an hour of fast trotting, they saw far ahead the glow of light from Jamin's sword. A short time later the four comrades were together again, moving in single file steadily northward through the night.

12

Jamin's Story

All that night and all the next day they traveled, stopping only long enough to eat. Late in the evening, they reached the cleft in the rock. Here they stopped to rest and sleep. They had not been attacked again during their rapid march, though once their swords had told them that enemy scouts were near.

But at the cleft of the rock they could rest without fear. They slept, and ate, and slept again. And during the quiet hours between sleep, they talked over their recent adventures. Wavor told them of how he had been captured and made to march, blindfolded and with his hands tied, all the way to castle despair.

"There," he said, "they threw me into the dungeon where you found me. I was given food which contained some sort of drug which weakened me. And twice daily one of the chiefs of the evil ones would visit me and tell me terrible false-hoods about the King and the brotherhood. He told me that, because of my failure at the out-post, my name had been stricken from the roll of the King's soldiers, and that nothing would be done, now or ever, to rescue me. Even though I knew it could not be true, I was on the point of believing it after a while."

"What a terrible thing," burst out Lanus. "Jamin, why do the King's soldiers not march in a body and destroy this castle despair and all who live in it?"

"We cannot," said Jamin from his seat against the cave wall. "We have not the strength, nor is that our mission. The King has given us the weap-ons to resist and defeat the enemy whenever and wherever we meet him, but it is decreed that the castles of evil will remain until the King returns to reign. Then He will lead us against these strong-holds and conquer them once and for all. In the meantime, these enemies are to test us, so that we will learn how to use the King's weapons."

Robin, who had been lying full-length on the cave floor, raised himself on his elbow. "Jamin," he said, "you told us that once you too had been imprisoned in castle despair. Will you tell us about it?"

"Yes, I will," said Jamin, "for you may perhaps learn by my mistakes."

He stretched his short legs out before him, leaned back comfortably against the wall, and began.

"As a young soldier, I was sometimes lazy. One summer day while on a mission for the King down in the valley, I fell asleep under a tree." (Here Jamin looked at Lanus, and that young man, remembering his own shortcomings, blushed deeply.) "When I awoke it was after dark, and I had been bound hand and foot by a group of the enemy. They had taken my sword and shield from me, and were carrying me on their shoulders.

"First they took me to castle doubt, which stands in an area of quicksand at the edge of the valley. Here they stuffed me with strange fruits in an effort to make me dissatisfied with my memories of the King's food. They also brought to my cell men who claimed to be former soldiers of the King who had seen 'the error of their ways.' These persons told me how much happier they had been since leaving the King's service (I have since learned that none of them were ever truly soldiers) and tried to convince me to renounce my allegiance.

"After some weeks in this castle, the enemy took me to castle despair, where I was put in the same cell Wavor occupied. Here they told me I would stay until I agreed to turn from the King and serve them. They promised me that if I would turn to their side, they would send me farther down the valley to castle unbelief, where (they said) were all manner of pleasures, and I should live at my ease for the rest of my life.

"I grew more and more discouraged as time went on, and several times thought of taking my own life. Then one day my chief tormentor came to my cell with another of the evil ones. They had with them, in addition to their own weapons, my sword and shield. Evidently the evil ones had been curious about our weapons. After getting mine into their hands, they had tried to see how they were used. But in the hands of the enemy, the shield immediately became tarnished, and the sword was dull and pointless. So they brought them to my cell to show me how much inferior they were to their own weapons.

" 'See how tarnished they are,' they said. 'We have tried to cut with the sword and have found that it is no good at all. Men armed with swords like this can never conquer us. Turn from this foolish soldiering, and join the ranks of evil!'

"Then I saw my opportunity. I was weak and sick, and they were two against one, but if I could get my hands on the sword perhaps the King would give me strength to strike! I told them I did not believe that the blade was dull, and asked them to show me. One of them drew the edge across a piece of cloth, holding the sword close so that I could see in the flickering light of the candle.

"I lifted my heart in a silent prayer for strength. Then, with all the effort I could muster, I threw myself forward, seizing the sword away from him. In my hand it came to life! Before he could recover, I thrust the sword into his heart. As he fell, I snatched the shield of faith. Then the other one hurled himself on me, and we battled back and forth across the narrow room. In my weak condition I would soon have been overcome, but the sword and shield fought for me, seeming to lift themselves, until finally my tormentor fell.

"I rested, trembling from weakness. There was no sound from outside the locked door. None of the others had heard. But I had no way to break out. Then it was that I noticed that the keyhole in the dungeon door was the same size and shape as my sword blade, and I tried thrusting the blade through it. The dungeon door opened! As I began wandering through passages looking for a way of escape, I found that my sword, which I carried drawn in my hand, was leading me forward. I followed, and found the same side door by which we entered the castle to rescue Wavor. In this lock my sword worked again, and I was able to strike down the guard and escape across the causeway.

"So you see," concluded Jamin, smiling, "why I was chosen to lead this expedition. Even our failures as soldiers of the King can be sometimes used to help others who have fallen in the same snare. Remember that, Wavor, and you too, Lanus. Be thankful for deliverance from failure, and be quick to help others who fail."

Jamin and Lanus sat together in silence for a while after the others were asleep. Lanus, with his knees drawn up beneath his chin, was thinking over the events of the past few days. Finally he said, "Jamin, there is one thing that is troubling me."

"What is it?"

"The face of one of the evil ones. Do you remember several months ago when I told you of going out with a rescue party into the forest and having my first bout with the enemy? Well, I remembered that evil one well. He was one of the largest that I have seen, and he looked at me with eyes filled with hate.

"That fight ended before either of us had touched the other, but the other night I saw him again. I am sure now that it was he who knocked me into the lake. Afterward he was in the forefront of the battle on the causeway and again in the ravine. I wounded him, but could not kill him. And now as I think of him it comes to me that he was also one of the two who attacked Robin and me on the night when I came to the castle for the first time. Jamin, why do I continue to meet this same fiend?"

Jamin's face was sober. "Your meeting was no accident, my boy. Many of the King's soldiers have a single evil one which pursues them. The name of your enemy is Besetting Sin. And what the weakness in your life which he attacks may be, only you know. You may wound him often, and you can always, if you use your sword and shield aright, beat him in each encounter, but you may never succeed in destroying him.

"He is not an adversary to be despised. He will grow more skilled in attacking you as you grow skilled in defeating him. He will learn your own strokes with the sword and use them against you. Only rarely does one of the King's soldiers com- pletely succeed in ridding himself of a Besetting Sin, and that after years of effort. So watch for him; don't be afraid of him, for through the sword of the spirit you can win the victory. And at last, when the King comes again, your adversary will fall forever in that final battle, for so has the King promised."

With a final friendly pat on Lanus's shoulder, Ja- min rolled himself in his cloak and slept. But Lanus sat long with his chin cupped in his hand, thinking of what he had heard.

13

Wavor's Great Test

During the period of rest at the cleft of the rock, Wavor gained strength rapidly. Fresh air, sleep, good food, water from the spring, the company of his fellow soldiers, and the presence of his beloved sword by his side, all combined to bring back spring to his step and strength to his arm.

They stayed there three days. "I want to give Wavor a chance to get as strong as possible," Jamin told Lanus. "You see, we can expect more trouble from the enemy between here and the castle. If we could have come straight through without stopping we might have reached the castle gates without further attack, but Wavor was too weak for that."

"What makes you sure they will attack us again?" asked Lanus.

"One is never sure about the enemy, Lanus, but

it is not likely that he will let a captive get away without a further try."

It was early on the third day when the little party finally left the high pinnacle and entered the shadows of the forest below. They traveled single file, Jamin first, then Wavor, then Lanus, with Robin bringing up the rear. They moved rapidly, without stopping, their shields ready on their left arms and their swords drawn in their hands. And, to avoid possible ambushes, Jamin led them by little-known paths.

But it seemed that there was little reason for caution. Mile after mile dropped behind, and the forest remained quiet and peaceful. Perhaps, Lanus thought, the enemy had given up after all. Perhaps the evil ones thought that they were already safe in the King's castle or perhaps they were watching other paths. But Jamin, leading the little group, still moved warily, flicking his eyes constantly from side to side over the ground in front of them, and looking carefully at each boulder or thicket which might conceal an enemy.

Early in the afternoon the trail dipped downward into a shadowy woodland, where it wound between giant boulders. Then it turned upward again, following the course of a narrow valley where the shadows were deep. As they neared a bend of the path, Jamin suddenly motioned them to stop. Lanus, looking ahead over Wavor's shoulder, saw that the light cast by Jamin's sword was flaring brightly.

They listened, but all was still. Not even the usual bird and insect noises were heard. After a moment, at Jamin's signal, they moved forward again. Slowly, their muscles tense, the little party approached the bend of the path, making as little noise as possible. As they rounded the turn, Lanus drew in his breath sharply. Ahead, the path sloped upward between two large rocks. And there, standing on the shadowed path between the boulders, tall and sinister, was one of the enemy!

He was dressed in black armor, with a huge black sword bare in his right hand, and he stood quietly, waiting, as motionless as one of the rocks themselves. Jamin turned to the others.

"Here our trouble begins," he said quietly. "Follow close behind me while I clear this one out of the way, then watch out for attacks from the side and rear."

He started forward, but Wavor, who had been staring, white-faced, at the sinister figure, suddenly whispered, "Wait! Wait, Jamin, I beg of you. I know who this is and why he is here!"

Jamin halted, still with a watchful eye on the enemy, and Wavor moved to his side.

"That is the evil one who captured me, and who tormented me daily in my cell at castle despair," said Wavor, trembling. "He has come to take me back with him."

"I'll take care of him," said Jamin, preparing to start forward again.

"No," said Wavor, "you do not understand. He it was who told me that even if I had had my sword that night, he still would have beaten and captured me. And I told him that the King's sword could vanquish him on any field!" He seized Jamin's shoulder. "Don't you see, that is why he is here alone—to prove my words. If you drive him away now, he will rise up before me in every battle hereafter. I must beat him singlehanded or die in the attempt!"

Jamin slowly lowered his sword. "Perhaps you are right, lad," he said softly. "We can break through and carry you to the castle, but until you yourself, with the King's weapons, win the victory over that which enslaved you, it will be an empty triumph. Go, and may our Lord and King guide your arm. We will keep watch, for other evil ones are certainly about."

As the three watched breathlessly, Wavor, his face pale but set and determined, moved forward alone along the path. As he did so, his opponent too, matching him step for step, came forward from between the rocks into the lighter shadow of the trees. When only a few paces separated them, they stopped and stood facing each other for a moment.

Neither spoke, but from the slopes around them the high-pitched wailing sound rose. A cloud darkened the valley, and a clammy chill fell across the place like the chill of the valley of despair. Then above the wail of evil rang the clear, beautiful notes of Wavor's trumpet, and his sword flashed as he leaped forward to the attack.

It was the most furious duel that Lanus had yet seen. The huge black sword of the enemy swung in a whistling arc, clashing blow after blow against Wavor's shield of faith. And Wavor struck out in return. Toe to toe they stood, each swaying with the force of the blows striking them, but neither giving ground. Then Wavor seemed to tire. He was forced backward one step, then two. Lanus and Robin would have rushed forward, but Jamin shook his head.

"He must finish it alone," he said.

A furious, overhand blow got past Wavor's shield and struck his left shoulder at a joint of his armor, wounding him. The force of the blow drove Wavor to his knees and the enemy, with a snarl of hate, leaped forward, raining blows on the upraised shield of the King's soldier. Lanus groaned. But, with a burst of almost superhuman strength, Wavor fought his way again to his feet, reeling under the blows of the relentless black sword. For a moment he stood, gathering strength for another effort, then, "For the King!" cried Wavor.

He lunged forward recklessly, swinging his sword in a great, two-handed stroke which caught the enemy by surprise and drove his shield in against his body. Again the sword flashed, and this time it sheared through shield and armor. For the third time Wavor's sword whistled through the air, and the evil one slumped to the path, his sword clattering loosely on the stones.

For an instant the three watchers stood motionless, stunned by the suddenness with which the end had come, while Wavor, his breath coming in deep sobs, leaned heavily on his sword above the body of his enemy. Then Jamin said, "Forward, quickly!" and sprang to Wavor's side. And with Lanus and Robin supporting the wounded soldier on either side, the little party rushed through the defile between the rocks.

They were none too quick, for the wailing noise had grown louder, and from the slopes others of the enemy left their hiding places behind trees and bushes and rushed toward the path to intercept them. Quickly the three formed in a tight, defensive knot with Wavor in the center and, as they beat back the attacks of the enemy, moved step by step up the path toward the open ridge.

It was a long struggle, but not a hopeless one.

There were not many evil ones in the group guarding this path, and they seemed confused and disheartened at the loss of their leader. As the fight neared the sunlit summit, the enemy's attacks slackened and, when they finally broke out into the sunlight, the last of the enemy dropped away down the slope. Jamin led the way along the ridge until he felt it was safe to rest, then while the others stood guard, he examined Wavor's wound.

"A deep cut, but not too serious," he said, washing the wound carefully with the water which he had brought from the cleft of the rock. Then, to Lanus's surprise, Jamin drew his sword and gently touched the flat of the blade to the still-bleeding wound. Seeing Lanus's astonished face, Jamin smiled.

"There is no end to the wonders of the sword, Lanus, as I told you before. What is death to the enemy is life and healing to the soldier of the King. The touch of the sword prevents infection of the wound, and starts it mending. See, the bleeding has stopped!"

And Wavor, sitting on the ground, said, "It feels better already, Jamin. I believe I'm strong enough to travel again."

"We'll rest a little longer while I bind up your wound," decided Jamin. "It is reasonably safe here, and we have plenty of time to get to the castle before nightfall. I think we may have seen the last of the enemy for today."

When the wound was bound, Jamin again led the way along the ridge toward home. His guess proved to be right for, though they kept a sharp lookout, they saw no more of the enemy. A few hours later, they came in sight of the familiar castle gates, and soon afterward were enjoying rest and food in the friendly warmth of the castle hall.

*　　*　　*

That evening, Lanus stood again in his own room. It seemed a long time since he had seen that room, though in reality it had been less than two weeks. But Lanus had changed during that time. He had seen and done many things. In particular he had learned the truth of those words which Jamin had quoted before the mission had begun: *"There is no restraint with the Lord to save by many or by few."*

Lanus took off his shield and hung it up. Then he saw something which made him forget his weariness—something which he had been far too busy to notice during the past days and nights. His shield of faith, which had been so drab and lusterless, had taken on a bright, gleaming surface. He remembered what Gayne had told him in the armory long ago: "These are strange and wonderful shields, Lanus. The shields made by men get scratched and nicked and dull with use, but the more these are used the brighter they shine!"

Each blow, each thrust, caught by the shield in the past days must have made it shine a little brighter. Now it was as bright as any in the castle!

Lanus's eyes lit with joy. The gleaming shield alone was reward enough for all the weary days and nights. To Lanus it was proof that he had made up for his failure in the King's service. It was a "well done" from the King Himself!

14

Back to the Valley

The safe return of the party was a cause of much rejoicing in the King's castle. Jamin told the story of Wavor's courageous battle, and that young man was received with open arms and restored to his former responsibilities. As for Robin and Lanus, they were besieged with questions by the young men of the castle, and had to tell many times over their adventures in the valley of despair.

Lanus found that the chain of outposts guarding the castle had been strengthened during their absence, and that two new outposts had been added to the group. Trees had been felled along the path to the valley, making the steep way down the mountainside more open and easier to patrol. But the enemy had been busy, and constant scrimmages occurred around the outposts and on the dark mountain slopes.

Robin was given charge of one of the new smaller outposts, and Lanus saw little of him. Lanus dropped contentedly back into his job of helping Jamin about his business of the castle. But he found himself called out more and more to form a part of rescue parties or reinforcements for some hard-pressed patrol or outpost. Frequently, on these occasions, he found himself the leader of small rescue parties, with a group of young soldiers under his command.

More than once, he found himself face to face with the particular enemy whom Jamin called his Besetting Sin, but each time his good sword and splendid condition gave him the victory. Lanus learned more about his enemy in the encounters. He found that if he struck out boldly, carrying the fight to the evil one, victory was easy, but that when he fought more cautiously, letting the enemy attack first, the evil one grew strong and was only defeated after a long and hard struggle.

One morning, several months after their return from the valley of despair, Lanus and Jamin were walking back to the castle after their daily sword practice, when Jamin said suddenly: "Lanus, have you thought of returning to the valley?"

"Back to my old life?" asked Lanus in amazement. "No, never!"

"I didn't mean that exactly," returned Jamin with a smile. "I mean, have you thought of bringing others to the castle in the same way that Robin brought you?"

Lanus studied the ground thoughtfully. "Yes, I have," he said at last. "I've thought of it, but I haven't done anything about it. Do you think I should go?"

Jamin looked at him soberly. "The King's last command to His soldiers before He left the valley was to tell others of Him."

Lanus sighed deeply. "The King must have directed you to speak to me today," he said. "To tell you the truth, Jamin, I have felt for several weeks now that I must go to the valley. The sword has been drawing me. Each time that I pass near the path in the course of my duties, the sword has pulled me toward it, and I have known in my inmost heart that it was the will of the King to send me. But each time I have refused to go. Jamin, perhaps I am foolish, but do you know, I am much more afraid of telling my old friends about the King than I am of meeting the enemy in open combat?"

"It is difficult for all of us," said Jamin kindly. "Being laughed at is one of the hardest things for any man to face. But that too is our duty as soldiers of the King. Besides, Lanus, when the King leads through the sword, the mission is never in vain. We may see no results, but His will is always best."

"I suppose I've been selfish," said Lanus, as they passed through the doorway into the castle. "There are many there in the valley who should know the King. I'll go, Jamin, as soon as I can!"

So Lanus went back to the valley.

It was a beautiful sunny morning when he left the castle and started down the rocky path. He wore a traveling cloak over his armor, and carried some of the King's food in a package by his side. He walked warily, looking from side to side into the woodland shadows for evidence of the enemy and, until he reached the open fields near the foot of the mountain, he carried his sword drawn in his hand. Then, knowing that the enemy was not likely to attack him in the open sunlight, he put it back into its sheath.

As he walked along, Lanus wondered how he would be received by his old friends. And he wondered too how he would feel when he found himself back in his boyhood haunts. Lanus had not, in all the many months at the castle, felt the least bit homesick for his old life in the valley, but still he wondered. . . .

As Lanus walked along the high road toward the village, thinking of these things, he suddenly became aware of a figure on the other side of the road, moving in the same direction as he himself was going. This sudden appearance startled Lanus, who had heard no one come up behind him. And he was even more startled when, looking more closely at this figure, he saw it to be one of the enemy!

Lanus whirled, drawing his sword and swinging his shield from his back to battle position on his left arm. But, as he did so the figure, grinning mockingly, drifted like a wraith of smoke up the bank on the side of the road. Lanus, puzzled and troubled, resumed his walk toward the village, but no sooner had he done so than the figure came down again to the road and walked parallel to him. Again Lanus turned to attack it, and again the leering face of the enemy retreated, but each time that he turned his face in the direction of the village, his enemy moved with him.

Then Lanus understood. This evil one was not sent to fight with him but to follow him on his mission in the valley. Resolutely, but with one eye cocked carefully on his enemy, he set out again toward the village.

The road toward the village ran past the homestead of Farmer Pelon, a man whom Lanus knew only slightly. He was about to pass it by when he felt the gentle pull of the sword. "The King wants me to turn in here," he said to himself. "I wonder why?" Obediently he left the high road and started up the path toward the house. Halfway there, he found his friend Ertel leaning against the fence. Ertel was a young man with whom Lanus had grown up, and he was as amazed to see Lanus as Lanus had been to see Robin a year or so before. In answer to his questions Lanus told him of the great change that had come into his life.

"Do you mean, Lanus," Ertel asked, "that you have given your life to the cause of fighting against evil?"

"I am a follower of the King," said Lanus, "who is the enemy of all that is evil."

"That is wonderful," said Ertel with real feeling. "I really believe, Lanus, that you have made a good and wise choice, and I admire you for it. I am not learned in the teaching of your King, and I know some speak evil of Him and of His followers, but I believe that His way will triumph in the end."

"I am glad you think as I do," said Lanus, greatly encouraged. "Will you come with me and see for yourself what our castle and fellowship are like?"

Ertel turned his eyes away and looked out across the fields of ripening grain. "I would like to," he said slowly, "but I can't. You see, Farmer Pelon has promised me a part interest in his crop if I help him cultivate and harvest it this year. With the money I receive, I plan to buy an acre or two of my own."

He looked at Lanus earnestly. "This opportunity means much to me, Lanus, and I can't afford to let anything spoil it. I cannot even spend a day away from my work, or I might be the loser."

"But don't you see," urged Lanus, "this is even more important. No farms nor lands nor crops should prevent you from finding truth!"

But Ertel only shook his head. Then Lanus saw, leaning against the fence only a short distance away, the dark figure of the enemy, smiling in ugly triumph at him. Quickly Lanus drew his sword and pointed it at the evil one!

"Look, Ertel, quickly! Do you not see at the edge of the field that evil thing, the curse of this valley? See how the power of the sword makes it visible? That is a part of the evil which rules over your land and your crops and, yes, your life. Will you not break away now, and come with me to freedom?"

But Ertel said, "I see nothing but the sun shining on the fields of wheat, ripening them for harvest."

So Lanus sadly bade him goodbye and went on toward the village, with the evil one drifting silently along on the other side of the road. Next the sword led him to a large house at the edge of the village, where lived Zemla, a long-time friend of Lanus's father, and a man who had always been kind to Lanus. Zemla, a thin, pleasant-faced man, sat writing at a desk piled with papers, but he laid down his pen with an eager smile when Lanus was announced.

"Lanus, my boy, do come in," he said. "I've been thinking of you much lately and wondering where you were. It has been more than a year since you last stopped in to talk to me. Where have you been and what have you been doing?"

Lanus told him of his adventures and how he had become a servant and soldier of the King.

142

Zemla listened quietly, his face expressionless. When Lanus had finished he said: "Ah, my boy, but you left the valley at the wrong time. When you left, we were having a bad year. The crops were poor, the people discontented, and we were on the verge of war with two of the other villages of the valley. Now we've changed all that. The village has developed a new fertilizer which will improve the output of the farms. We've changed our mayor and village council, and things are going much better. And the threat of war is just about over. I'm serving right now as part of a commission which is drafting a peace treaty with the other villages. If we design this treaty properly we need never have another war."

Lanus remembered the words of the King's book in the castle library: *"They shall cry peace, peace, when there is no peace. . . ."* But he thought it best not to argue that point. So he said: "I left the valley, not for those things you mention, but because I wanted to be free of sin and to find truth and righteousness. This I found in the service of the King. Zemla, the King's service is the only way to true happiness."

But Zemla said, shaking his head, "Lanus, I am older than you, and wiser. The way you follow has attracted many in the past, but we are more enlightened now, and we solve our problems right here in the valley instead of trying to escape from them.

"Listen, Lanus, I had a friend when I was your age who thought as you do. He was a brilliant lad and well might have been a wise and useful man. But he chose to throw his life away following that foolish idea of your King, and chasing phantoms on the mountainside. His name was Jamin."

"I know him," said Lanus simply.

"Don't be like him, Lanus. Stop before it is too late. Believe me, this myth of an evil power which hangs over the valley is all nonsense. There is no evil which we cannot do away with ourselves. And, when peace is finally brought to the entire valley, you will find that these fairy tales of evil beings will disappear."

Lanus looked past Zemla through the open window and saw, under the tree in the front yard, the mocking figure of his enemy, who stood listening to the conversation. And he thought sadly of the wise men of the world, like Zemla, who for all their wisdom cannot see the figure of evil for what it is, and who try to fight it with laws and treaties, not with the King's sword.

Lanus sighed and rose to his feet. "I will never return to my old life, Zemla," he said. "I believe that Jamin made the wise choice, and you the unwise one. And I earnestly invite you to visit our castle and judge for yourself."

Zemla smiled. "I should like to come sometime, Lanus, if only to humor you and to see Jamin again, but I'm much too busy now working for peace. However, come and see me again, on your next trip to the valley."

Lanus left the house and walked on through the village, sad and disheartened. He was failing in his mission. When he again looked up, he found himself in front of the home of Farmer Broadleaf, where there had always, in time past, been a welcome for him.

For several moments he stood there before he realized that the sword was gently pulling him toward the entrance. The good farmer and his wife were overjoyed to see him again, as were the

Broadleaf children. But when Lanus asked how his friends had been getting along since he last saw them, the farmer shook his head.

"Rather poorly, Lanus," he said. "My crop last year failed, leaving me in debt. This year crops are better and would enable me to pay my debt, but I have not enough money to hire the help I need to harvest it. If only I had one more to work with me. . . ."

Lanus hesitated. There was nothing he wanted so much as to leave the valley again and return to the castle, but he could not leave his friend in trouble. "I will stay and help you for a few weeks," he said.

15
Call of the Silver Trumpet

So Lanus worked in Farmer Broadleaf's fields, and stayed as a guest at Farmer Broadleaf's house. Day after day in the hot sun he worked. And during the evenings, in the large cheerful kitchen of the farmhouse, Lanus told his friends about the King and His castle. The farmer and his wife and his three small sons listened earnestly and asked many questions. Lanus on his part was glad of the chance to talk of his King.

Many times during the course of those evening talks, Lanus had an opportunity to point out how the King desired men to come to Him and become His followers. He would, on these occasions, ask the farmer and his wife to visit the castle with him as he had asked his other friends. But neither Farmer Broadleaf nor his wife would give him a definite answer. They were interested; they wanted to come, Lanus was sure, but they would not promise.

Best of all on these evenings, Lanus enjoyed talking to the Broadleaf children. They would gather around, asking him questions about his life at the castle, and listening openmouthed to his answers. Two of the three boys wanted to hear of nothing over and over again but battles and adventures. But Henda, a thin quiet lad who was the middle one of the three in point of age, was different. He listened eagerly to every detail that Lanus spoke about the King and His castle and the King's great book, and would sit by the hour with burning eyes fixed on Lanus's face, asking him questions and more questions.

And so the weeks went by. Each day, Lanus polished his weapons and longed for the time when he could return to the King's castle, but always it seemed that there was work still to be done that could not be handled by the farmer alone.

Finally it seemed that the end had been nearly reached. Most of the harvest had been gathered in, and what was left could easily be done by Farmer Broadleaf himself. Wood had been cut and stored for the winter, and enough food had been brought into the roomy basement of the farmhouse to last the family through the cold season. Lanus decided he could stay no longer. But before he could tell Farmer Broadleaf of his plans, the call came! It was nearly noon, and Lanus was working shoulder to shoulder with Farmer Broadleaf in the sun-warmed fields when, suddenly, in the distance, he heard the trumpet call. He raised his head and listened. There it was again! Faint and far away, it was nevertheless unmistakably the sound of the silver trumpet.

Lanus dropped his scythe. "Farmer Broadleaf, the King is calling and I must return to the castle."

The farmer nodded his grizzled head. "I have been fearing that you might leave us soon," he said. "When must you go?"

Lanus lifted his eyes to the ridge of the great mountains, where the sun glinted on the distant castle turret just visible over the trees. Once again, the trumpet call floated faintly down the wind.

"Now," he said.

Farmer Broadleaf sighed. "Very well," he said. "I will go back with you to the house while you gather your belongings."

The whole Broadleaf family was gathered in the kitchen when Lanus came down from his bedroom, ready to leave. Lanus crossed the room and stood before the farmer and his wife.

"I wish you and your family would come to the castle too," he said.

"We have talked many times about it," said the farmer, looking at the floor, "but we are old and rooted here."

"You can never be too old to come to the King," answered Lanus, and Mrs. Broadleaf's eyes filled suddenly with tears.

"Perhaps, husband," she said softly, "if Lanus will return for us, in a few weeks we can go to the castle, at least on a visit. I want very much to go."

Farmer Broadleaf hesitated a moment, then nodded his head. But then the boy Henda came from the corner of the fireplace and stood before his parents.

"I want to go now!" he said. "I want to be a soldier of the King, and go with Lanus. May I?"

The farmer and his wife looked at each other for

a long moment. Then the farmer said hesitantly, "If the boy really wants to go, we must let him. We can trust Lanus to take care of him."

And so it was that when Lanus, a few moments later, left the farmer's house and started down the high road toward the great mountains, young Henda went with him. Mr. and Mrs. Broadleaf and the other two children stood at the gate to see them go.

"Wait for me," called Henda over his shoulder to his mother and father. "I will come back soon with Lanus and take you to the castle."

Lanus and Henda walked rapidly down the high road, and by late afternoon reached the slopes of the great mountains. As the sun went down and twilight began, Lanus imagined that a faint, disquieting chill crept into the air. It disturbed him and, long before they reached the shadows of the woods, he had drawn his sword and slung his shield into ready position.

The woods, like the fields below, were peaceful, but the chill persisted. It was a vague, penetrating cold, and reminded Lanus forcibly of the atmosphere of the valley of despair.

"Something is wrong," he muttered to himself, and redoubled his watchfulness as he pressed forward. No enemy appeared, but it was not until the last turn was rounded and the castle gates came into view that Lanus relaxed his vigilance.

The gate was opened by one of the youngest of the King's soldiers. When they were safely inside, Lanus turned to him. "Can you tell me where to find Jamin? I would like to report to him at once."

"He's in the field with the rest. There are only a few of us here guarding the castle."

"Is the trouble that serious?" asked Lanus anxiously.

"It is very serious. The enemy has gotten between us and the valley. I don't know how you managed to get up the path. The evil ones have been massing their forces to attack us for some time. We knew that, but we didn't know where the blow would come. Today, they attacked us from the valley, overran the ridge, and captured the tower above the path. This evening they began pushing toward the castle. Jamin is leading our forces."

"Jamin! Where is Latta? And Gayne?"

"Latta has been very ill for several weeks, and cannot leave his bed. Gayne was badly wounded in the enemy's first attack, and lies in the castle."

Lanus stood staring at the other lad for a moment, while the full meaning of what was said dawned on him. Then he wheeled toward the gate.

"Let me out!" he said crisply, "and look after Henda here until I return. Make him comfortable and welcome. I must go to Jamin!"

Once again the gate swung open and Lanus, sword in hand, darted out into the night.

16
For the King!

Lanus moved swiftly out along the ridge which extended out into the valley above the path. The tree-covered top of the ridge was broad and gently rolling. From the castle wall the ground sloped gently upward to a crest of a low rise, then dipped into a small valley. Then it rose again on a long slope to the wind-swept tip of the ridge where the stone tower was located. As Lanus crossed the little valley at a trot, he saw halfway up this slope the glow of his comrades' swords stretched in a battle line under the trees.

The line was quiet as he approached. Lanus made his way toward the center of the line, where he knew Jamin would be. And there he found him standing under a tree with a small group of soldiers. Jamin greeted him warmly but soberly.

"I'm glad you're back," he said. "It looks as

though we'll need every sword tonight."

"What is the situation?" asked Lanus breathlessly.

"We are not sure exactly," said Jamin slowly. "It is not just a local attack. For the first time, our enemies have found a way up the cliffs from the valley and, this afternoon, swept over the tower with nearly their whole strength. Of course they now control the path as well. We've stopped them here on the ridge only with difficulty, and I expect another attack in a few minutes. We've drawn as many men as we can from the castle and from the outposts, and we will try to hold them at this point."

Just then there was a stir in the battle line, and Jamin said, "Get ready, Lanus, quickly! They are coming again. You will fight beside me for the time being."

He turned away and called an order. Lanus just had time to take off his traveling cloak when the trumpet sounded again and the flaring of swordlights along the line told them that the enemy was advancing. At the same time the now familiar wailing sound was heard, but louder and more terrifying than Lanus had ever heard it.

Then came the evil ones. They seemed larger than they had ever been, and they were armed with heavy, flaming darts. They came forward with a rush among the trees, striking the King's line along its whole length and driving it backward down the slope.

"For the King!" cried Jamin leaping in to rally his men, and, with a shout, the line held again. Lanus went into battle at Jamin's side and found himself set upon by two of the evil ones. But as he was driven backward another of the King's soldiers appeared at his side and together they repelled the attack. Then the King's men surged forward in a countercharge, and the line of battle swung back again nearly to where it had been before. But more and more of the enemy strength was thrown into the fray, and once again Jamin and his men were forced backward through the trees toward the small valley.

Never had Lanus been in a battle of such fierceness. The minutes stretched into hours, and still the fight raged, with the weary soldiers of the King battling ever fresh waves of enemy reinforcements. Back and forth surged the battle line, but the backward movements were always the longer, so that, as the night wore on, the King's men were pushed, foot by foot, across the little valley and up the rise overlooking the castle itself.

As the morning mist began to form on the slopes, there was a lull in the fighting. Lanus, panting with weariness, leaned on his sword and looked over the field. The line was thinner now and there were many gaps where brave men had fallen. But the ground in front was carpeted with the bodies of their enemies. Lanus looked at the face of the soldier who had been fighting next to him, and saw with surprise that it was Robin. The two friends smiled at each other wearily.

"Where did Jamin go?" asked Lanus.

"He went to the left to steady the line," said Robin. "Here he comes now."

Jamin's armor was stained, his face was gray and tired, and he had been wounded slightly on the left arm, but he smiled at the two lads as calmly as though nothing were wrong.

"They will be at us again in a few moments," he said, answering their unspoken question. "They have just stopped to regroup. There is no question about it, this is their whole army and an all-out attack. I have called for the detachment guarding our rear to join us in our stand here, as well as the few soldiers left in the castle. We must hold them on this hill."

"What is the enemy's plan, Jamin?" asked Lanus.

"They must mean to drive us back against the castle walls and destroy us entirely," said Jamin in a matter-of-fact voice. "We could save ourselves now by withdrawing into the castle, but then they would hold both the ridge and the path to the valley. And it is our duty to keep the way open to the valley until the King comes again, so that others may come to know Him."

Robin, who had been peering through the mist, said quietly, "Here they come again!"

Swordlights were flaring high along the King's line, and the grim-faced soldiers were closing their ranks and tightening their battle harnesses for a determined stand. Then up through the mist with their wailing cry came the evil ones, rank on rank, under cover of a shower of darts. As the main assault struck the King's line, still another force attacked from the side, so that the line of soldiers was forced backward in a curve.

For a long moment of furious hand-to-hand fighting the line held, strengthened by the small garrison from the castle which just then came into the fight. But then the sheer weight of numbers began to tell. Lanus felt himself being driven backward to the very crest of the rise. Then, in spite of Jamin's heroic efforts to rally them, the King's soldiers, still fighting fiercely, were swept over the crest and down the slope toward the castle wall!

There, against the wall, the retreat stopped, for there was nowhere else to go. This was the final stand! With backs against the wall and shields close in front of them, the soldiers of the King stood, prepared to fight to the last man. No room was there to swing their swords; it was the point or nothing, so they thrust and parried and thrust again until their arms were numb with weariness. Lanus and Robin fought shoulder to shoulder, silently but with grim determination. Next to them stood Jamin, his tireless sword flashing out terrible retaliation against foe after foe. Farther down the line, standing firm as the very stones of the wall itself, were Jon and Wavor and Del.

How long they stood there, beating off charge after charge of the desperate enemy, Lanus never knew. But finally, just as he began to feel that he could no longer hold up his weapons, the pressure slackened. The evil ones were withdrawing! A moment later the last of the attackers had gone and the area along the wall was quiet, except for the sobbing gasps of the exhausted soldiers.

Lanus slumped weakly to the ground at the foot of the wall. He was bleeding from several cuts which he had not even felt in the heat of battle. And neither Robin nor Jamin was in better condition. As the beaten, helpless remnants of the King's army rested, the first streaks of gray morning light touched the castle turrets.

In front of them the white morning mist now shrouded the entire slope. Lanus stared into it, dazed and unseeing. Was this the end of the King's cause? Was it for this he had left the valley and entered the King's service? Was the road from the valley to freedom to be forever sealed to the Lanuses and Hendas and Farmer Broadleafs who wished for a better hope than the valley offered?

Suddenly Lanus became aware that the area near the top of the rise was becoming darker and more sinister. Black patches of fog appeared in strips, hanging like tattered curtains against the whiteness of the mist. It reminded him of something he had seen before somewhere. Painfully, his tired brain tried to recall it. Then in a flash he remembered—the black fog! The black deadly fog of the valley of despair!

He turned his head. Jamin was sitting a few feet away, his head buried in his hands. "Jamin, look! They've brought the blackness of darkness with them!"

Jamin raised his head and looked for a long moment up the slope to where the black curtains were spreading noiselessly across the hilltop. "So," he said at last, "that is the plan. They want not only to close the valley road, but to spread their own deadly atmosphere around the King's castle itself." He dropped his head again. "We must rest now, while we can," he said. "They will come once more to destroy us before the fog separates us from them completely."

Again Lanus sat silent, watching the fog. But his mind went back to the valley of despair and the fight against the forces of evil there. Then the three of them, Jamin and Robin and Lanus, had defeated the strongest of the evil ones in their own valley. Why was it now that the King's soldiers were beaten in the very shadow of the King's castle?

Lanus looked at his sword as it lay beside him. He recalled how, in the valley of despair, this blade had seemed to fight of its own accord, how it had led him forward, defending him against attack, and how it had sought out unerringly the weak point in his opponent's armor. Why was it that this same sword was being driven back in defeat?

Then the answer came to him.

The sword was not defeated. It was only men who had been driven backward, only men who had been beaten. Each stroke of the sword had been true and deadly, but the legs under it had faltered and given way.

No, the sword of the King was not defeated. It was still quick and powerful and sharper than any other. As long as earnest hearts and legs and arms would carry it forward, the sword of the spirit was—would ever be—invincible.

Lanus remembered how, in the King's great book, soldiers of the King had battled in days gone by. He remembered Paul, standing alone, sword in hand, while the city of Athens mocked. He remembered Daniel, who had stood with the sword against the forces of evil of his day. And he remembered Joshua, who in a time of great peril for the King's forces, had stood forth for the King with these words: *"Choose ye this day whom ye will serve . . . but as for me and my house, we will serve the Lord!"*

These were highpoints in the lives of the King's soldiers. These were times when the King strengthened them and guided their arms to victory. There were other times when, because of the weakness of man, the King's banners were driven back in defeat. But it was not for soldiers of the

King to question. The King, invisible, powerful, tender, and kind, was looking over the scene with His all-seeing eyes. The sword was the King's weapon. Lanus was only it bearer.

All this came to Lanus in an instant, as he sat looking at his sword. And he knew what his duty was. Lanus must stand for the King! And he would go forward! Under the eye of the King of kings he would, alone if necessary, carry the sword forward against the King's enemies so long as his legs would move!

Slowly, painfully, Lanus struggled to his feet. He was tired with a terrible weariness, and his legs and arms trembled, but he forced his body to stand upright, facing his enemies. He stood there, swaying, fighting for strength! He said no word, but several of the soldiers slumped nearby against the wall looked up at him wonderingly as he tightened his helmet strap with fumbling fingers and lifted his shield.

Then he raised the sword.

The hilt was warm to the touch—warmer than it had ever been, and the sword was feather-light. As he raised it, Lanus felt a strength that was not his own flowing into his limbs. And then something happened! The blade of the sword itself began to shine with a strange light as though it had been heated white hot in a furnace. Many times brighter than the usual glow which came from the sword was this shining, and it flashed from the blade like a flame of fire.

Beside him, he heard Robin struggling to his feet. "Jamin," cried Robin, "look! Look at Lanus's sword!"

Jamin raised his head. "The shining sword," he breathed. "I have seen it at last."

160

Slowly, as in a trance, Jamin rose and drew his own sword. And at once it too began to glow with a flaming light. Then Robin's shaking hand found his sword pommel, and a moment later a shining sword flashed in his hand as well. And all along the wall, startled faces of soldiers were turned toward the three as they stood in the unearthly light!

Jamin said, wondering, "Many times in the hands of men of old the sword has shone, but never have I heard of more than one shining at the same time."

And Lanus, his eyes glowing, answered, "It is our King's way of showing us that His sword will never fail, though heaven and earth pass away!"

All along the line now, tired soldiers were getting to their feet. And, as each man drew his sword, it began to shine until the whole line was aflame with a light that none had seen before. Then Jamin stepped out and turned to face his comrades.

"Soldiers of the King," he said simply, "let us go forward. Breathe against the blade when you pass through the black fog, then drive against the enemy with the point and the edge. And let us not stay our hands until the evil ones are driven over the cliffs at the end of the ridge."

There were no words in answer, but Lanus, looking down the line, saw tired faces lit with new strength and hope. Then Jamin turned toward the enemy and raised his sword.

And the silver trumpet sounded.

From end to end the whole line of shining swords, borne by the King's soldiers, surged out from the wall and forward up the hill. As they went, someone began singing one of the King's

161

marching songs. Other voices joined in and, in a moment, the praises of the King were rolling out in a great, swelling chorus. And Lanus, marching confidently forward, knew that the battle was already won—had been won from the instant when, casting self aside, he had truly dedicated his life to bearing the King's sword!

There might be other battles for Lanus, but it would not be Lanus who fought them. Battles would be fought and won by the King of kings—Lanus would only carry forward the King's sword. Perhaps, in one of those battles, the sword would again shine as a flame in Lanus's hand; perhaps not. That was not for him to know. He would march, as one of the vast number of nameless men, from ages past to age present, have marched—under the King's banner and bearing the ageless sword. For unto them the King has said: *"Go ye into all the world, and preach the gospel. . . . And, lo, I am with you alway, even unto the end of the age."*

*   *   *

Forward up the hill go the King's soldiers though the white mist swirls, blotting out the view. And we stand, you and I, in the gray light by the towering castle wall, and watch them go. Ahead of them hangs the black curtain of darkness, and beyond it waits the enemy. But the line of shining swords moves steadily on. And victory is in the sound of the tramping feet.

Somewhere near the center of that line (you and I can no longer tell in the mist which one he is) marches Lanus, young man of the valley, soldier of the King of kings and bearer of the King's own sword!

The Challenge

Stand therefore, having your loins girt about with truth, and having on the breastplate of righteousness; and your feet shod with the preparation of the gospel of peace; above all, taking the shield of faith, wherewith ye shall be able to quench all the fiery darts of the wicked. And take the helmet of salvation, and the sword of the spirit, which is the word of God: praying always with all prayer and supplication in the spirit.

From the New Testament
Ephesians 6:14-18